Selected

JAMES K. BAXTER was born in [ ]
and attended Quaker schools in Ne[ ]
he enrolled at the University of Otago and published his first collection of poetry, *Beyond the Palisade*. He abandoned his course a year later, struggling with alcoholism, and from 1945 to 1947 took a series of manual jobs. He was baptised as an Anglican, and in 1948 married Jacqueline Sturm and published a further collection of poetry, *Blow, Wind of Fruitfulness*. His third major collection, *The Fallen House*, was published in 1953. Baxter joined Alcoholics Anonymous in 1954, and was greatly influenced by its principles; he was also increasingly drawn to Roman Catholicism, and in 1958 was received into the Church. His collection *In Fires of No Return* (1958) brought him international recognition. A UNESCO Fellowship enabled him to travel to Japan and India. In 1966 he was awarded a Robert Burns Fellowship at the University of Otago. He wrote poetry, plays and works of criticism prolifically, but in 1968 he left his work and family to establish a drop-in centre for drug addicts in Auckland. A year later, he began to create a commune at Jerusalem (in Māori, Hiruharama), a former mission station. His collections *Jerusalem Sonnets* (1970), *Jerusalem Daybook* (1971) and *Autumn Testament* (1972) explore his experience of this period. Baxter died in Auckland in 1972 and was buried at Jerusalem in a funeral incorporating Catholic and Māori rites.

PAUL MILLAR is an Associate Professor of English at the University of Canterbury (Christchurch, New Zealand), with research interests in New Zealand, Australian, and Pacific literature. He previously lectured at Victoria University of Wellington, where he co-founded the New Zealand Electronic Text Centre. He has been an exchange professor and Fulbright scholar at the University of Hawai'i and was for some years a member of the board of the New Zealand Book Council. His books include the definitive account of Baxter's early development, *Spark to a Waiting Fuse* (2001), and the biography *No Fretful Sleeper: A Life of Bill Pearson* (2010), which received the prestigious Copyright Licensing Limited Writer's Award. Millar has twice judged the Montana New Zealand Book Awards.

FyfieldBooks aim to make available some of the great classics of British and European literature in clear, affordable formats, and to restore often neglected writers to their place in literary tradition.

FyfieldBooks take their name from the Fyfield elm in Matthew Arnold's 'Scholar Gypsy' and 'Thyrsis'. The tree stood not far from the village where the series was originally devised in 1971.

> Roam on! The light we sought is shining still.
> Dost thou ask proof? Our tree yet crowns the hill,
> Our Scholar travels yet the loved hill-side

from 'Thyrsis'

JAMES K. BAXTER

Selected Poems

Edited with an introduction by
PAUL MILLAR

Fyfield*Books*

CARCANET

Acknowledgements

My sincere thanks to Jacquie Baxter, John Baxter and the James K. Baxter Trust for consistent and generous support; to Geoff Miles for his invaluable contribution to both the selection and introduction; to Max Richards for perceptive advice; to my colleagues in the University of Canterbury English Programme for their friendship and interest; to Kay Nicholls for her meticulous proof reading and valuable comments; to Nigel Brown for the use of his striking Baxter image; and to my editors for their patience. I dedicate my small portion of this book to Kay, Aaron, Gareth and Lauren with love.

First published in Great Britain in 2010 by
Carcanet Press Limited
Alliance House
Cross Street
Manchester M2 7AQ

First published in New Zealand in 2010 by Auckland University Press,
University of Auckland, Private Bag 92019, Auckland 1142, New Zealand

Poems copyright © The James K. Baxter Trust

Selection and editorial matter copyright © Paul Millar 2010

The right of Paul Millar to be identified as the editor of this work
has been asserted by him in accordance with the
Copyright, Designs and Patents Act of 1988
All rights reserved

A CIP catalogue record for this book is available from the British Library
ISBN 978 1 84777 047 9

The publisher acknowledges financial assistance from Arts Council England

Supported by
**ARTS COUNCIL
ENGLAND**

Typeset by XL Publishing Services, Tiverton
Printed and bound in England by SRP Ltd, Exeter

Contents

Introduction

By 1972, when James K. Baxter died aged just forty-six, his colourful life and distinctive poetry had captured the imagination of New Zealanders as no literary figure before him. Part of this legacy was the curious possessiveness Baxter inspired amongst those who had had anything to do with him – even his detractors insisted on their version of Baxter. In the words of the critic Howard McNaughton: 'everyone seems to think that his bit of Baxter was the genuine stuff and that anything else is a cheap fraud'.[1] Still today many New Zealanders find Baxter an appealing, unsettling paradox – the non-conforming poet, profoundly critical of society, who remained intimately involved and invested in the processes he attacked. Baxter, who described himself with some accuracy as the 'sore thumb of the tribe,'[2] envisaged in 1966 a future where he was lodged in 'Mother New Zealand's' consciousness, 'perhaps a hundred years from now ... haunting her sleep, like something lost, like a voice whose owner one cannot quite identify, slipping in between the TV and the tranquillizers'.[3]

This idea of Baxter as a literary relic sunk deep in the New Zealand collective unconscious to disturb the nation's slumbers may help explain the fact that despite being one of the most prolific and precocious English-language poets of the twentieth century he is almost unknown outside his country. A non-New Zealander might reasonably suppose that a poet who was born and died in his own country, who left it only twice for around three years in total, and who eventually dropped out of mainstream society to found a rural commune based on Māori tribal principles (renaming himself 'Hemi' in the process), must have had little to give or take from the wider world. In fact the opposite is the case – scratch the surface of Baxter's life and it becomes immediately evident that for all the New Zealand referents and local content, his poetry is as firmly a product of twentieth-century global culture as the work of any poet one might name. Everything Baxter wrote was fashioned and defined by 'the winds of a terrible century' that distributed around the globe more profound change and upheaval than at any other period in human history.[4] His sense of identity was shaped by elements as diverse as the Scottish Highland clearances, nineteenth-century colonialism, British higher education, pacifist resistance to two world wars, immersion in the canons of classical myth and English literature, marriage to the Māori writer J.C. Sturm, recovery from alcoholism, conversion from Anglicanism to Catholicism (his observance of which seemed at times provocatively theatrical), witnessing extreme poverty in India, opposition to US foreign policy in Vietnam and the stark fact that in his lifetime humans had developed the capacity to destroy all life on earth.

Baxter's poetry is not the work of a writer from the literary periphery; it emerges from the centre of the body of world writing and is connected in ways profound and subtle to the work of other major poets. His yearning for pre-lapsarian paradise, for example, aligns him with the Romantics; his inherent resistance to dehumanising social structures merits comparison with Blake; his sensitivity to the numinous binds him to Hopkins; he empathised strongly with Dylan Thomas and emulated him by producing plays and verse drama; his confessional mode, influenced at first by Louis MacNeice's *Autumn Journal*, gained powerfully from exposure to Robert Lowell's *Life Studies*; his identification with 1960s counter-culture permits comparison with the likes of Allen Ginsberg and Jack Kerouac, and so on.

Beyond the Palisade (1944), Baxter's first book, was discovered by Allen Curnow, New Zealand's most influential critic, before its publication. Curnow, already a major poet, was then formulating a definition of authentic local poetry for his anthology *A Book of New Zealand Verse: 1923–45*. His thesis, which would dominate New Zealand literature in the second half of the twentieth century, was that the majority of the country's early versifiers unrealistically idealised settler experience. He sought a mode of writing vitally related to New Zealand experience through thematic preoccupation with the land, sea, voyaging, settler alienation and honest if dystopian depictions of a society afflicted by depression, isolation and war. It was a project informed by modernist sensibility and conditionally committed to a form of literary nationalism.

At the time it seemed that Baxter might be the youthful standard bearer capable of assuring this new nationalist poetic an authentic future. Curnow, who selected six poems from *Beyond the Palisade* while it was in the press, described Baxter's writing as: 'strong in impulse and confident in invention, with qualities of youth in verse which we have lacked; yet with a feeling after tradition and a frankly confessed debt (besides the unsought affinities) to some older New Zealand poets'. He asserted that since R.A.K. Mason in 1923, 'no New Zealand poet has proved so early his power to say and his right to speak'.[5] With a successful book and Curnow's endorsement, Baxter was transformed from a solitary adolescent into a figure of national acclaim ranked alongside such major local figures as Mason, A.R.D. Fairburn, Charles Brasch, Denis Glover and Curnow himself.

But there was a problem with Baxter's triumph; the poems Curnow selected for their authentic New Zealand content were at the time aberrations in Baxter's oeuvre. As much as Baxter himself valued a New Zealand landscape poem like 'The Mountains' (see p. 6), it wasn't representative of most of his verse, which was then a largely neo-Romantic amalgam of Blake, Hopkins and the English Pylon Poets, suffused with mythical themes and classical allusions expressing a complex personal and private symbolism. Right into his twenties Baxter was firmly sceptical about New Zealand poetry, seeing himself as a poet in the English tradition who happened to live in New Zealand. By the late 1940s his writing was more closely focused on New Zealand, but he never signed up to Curnow's project, and in subsequent years the two would become increasingly at odds.

By the 1960s Curnow, and those sympathetic to his aims, had lost patience with Baxter's production of poetry 'muffle[d] in literary tissue', displaying 'a throwback to the make-believe art of earlier generations'.[6] The most problematic 'literary tissue' was Baxter's ubiquitous layering of classical allusion, which appeared to many commentators as pretentious and elitist. In Baxter's defence, it was a mythical mode that belonged not to the public school classroom or the literary salon, but rather – in the spirit of twentieth-century students of myth like J.G. Frazer and Carl Jung – to the realm of the 'primitive', the natural, and the instinctive ... a direct route to the collective unconscious, a way of 'rediscovering [one's] own buried natural self'.[7]

There is another, more complicated, explanation for Baxter's differences with Curnow and various other poets than simply a disagreement over acceptable and authentic modes of poetic expression. It is connected to the fact that by the time of his death Baxter had in various ways fallen out with a large number of people, not just poets, who had once been close friends and supporters. To understand why it is necessary to go back to September 1939 when New Zealand locked step with Britain and declared war on Germany. For Baxter, who was only thirteen, it seemed as if the country had declared war on his family also. He knew his father had been a heroic pacifist in the First World War, and he had been moved and horrified by the torture his father had endured for his convictions at the hands of his own countrymen, disturbingly described by Archibald Baxter in his 1939 memoir *We Will Not Cease*: 'When I was only semen in a gland / Or less than that, my father hung / From a torture post at Mud Farm / Because he would not kill' (see p. 120). The Second World War saw the entire family harassed by authorities, shunned by neighbours, and Baxter's older brother Terence imprisoned indefinitely in defaulter's detention. For Baxter – bullied at school and isolated in his community – the poetry he wrote to fill his solitary adolescence was as much a form of self-protection as a precocious efflorescence.

It was in these hundreds of poems written between 1942 and 1946 that Baxter developed and refined an argument with conformity and the status quo that would dominate his life and his writing. While he considered the alienating experiences of adolescence 'very valuable, for they taught me to distrust mass opinion and sort out my own ideas', he also found them 'distinctly painful. I could compare them perhaps with the experiences of a Jewish boy growing up in an anti-Semitic neighbourhood. They created a gap in which the poems were able to grow.'[8]

An appreciation of this notion of the 'gap' is essential to any sustained reading of Baxter's poetry. As a teenager he began to conceive of the poetic self as a composite of opposites dwelling within in a state of perpetual poem-producing tension. In later life he often referred to his 'collaborator, my schizophrenic twin, who has always provided me with poems',[9] an anarchic other self, inhabiting 'the cellblock in the basement of my mind ... incorrigible, ineducable, unemployable'.[10] In an interview Baxter explained that a 'kind of tension of belief often lies behind the poems, and it leads to a certain edge'.[11] Such tension, he believed, underpinned his best poetry, and always at the locus of tension was some version of the gap – that paradoxical abyss from which poems originate. While versions of the gap recur in Baxter's writing, it is not a fixed symbol. It may be a site of absence within which to discover the true self; or a place of stillness where the mind is silenced and God is experienced. In the later poetry it becomes 'Wahi Ngaro: the void out of which all things come. That is my point of beginning. That is where I find my peace.'[12]

In Baxter's life this need for some form of the 'gap' saw him repeatedly identify a separation between his own ideas and the consensus of the dominant mindset. While he often appeared to ascribe to popular opinion, and was for many years a respectable family man and bureaucrat, for poetry's sake he strove to minimise his concessions to 'the Calvinist ethos which underlies our determinedly secular culture like the bones of a dinosaur buried in a suburban garden plot – work is good; sex is evil; do what you're told and you'll be all right; don't dig too deep into yourself'. By his own estimation he had not sold out, only traded 'as little as I can – the use of the hands and a little of the brain – like a woman in a brothel who merely serves food to the guests'.[13]

When one understands the extent to which Baxter believed that he wrote best when he was at odds with the status quo – that a life lived safely threatened his art – then apparently contradictory aspects of his behaviour and writing begin to make sense: his nonconformist stance while holding positions of responsibility within the structures he attacked; his preference for the wisdom of his father over the professorial knowledge of his grandfather while maintaining lifelong relationships with intellectuals; his scathing attacks on educators while training and working as a teacher and battling to complete a university degree; his profound renunciation of marriage, family and respectability to adopt the role of guru founder of a hippie commune on the Whanganui River – a move that was not the aberration some have painted it, but an almost inevitable return to the state of principled marginalisation that shaped him so powerfully in his teenage years.

Baxter's attraction to tightly knit groups that defy the mainstream had originated in adolescence. For the rest of his life he identified strongly with tribal manifestations – those distinctive communities

in which cohesion increases in response to persecution and alien-
ation – from the oppressed Highland clans of his Scottish forebears;
through pacifists, poets, alcoholics and Catholics (a minority in
predominately Protestant New Zealand), to the local Māori iwi
(kinship group), and Baxter's own commune, called by him 'Nga
Mokai', which means 'the fatherless ones', the tribes of the
Whanganui River settlement at Hiruharama (the Māori transliter-
ation of 'Jerusalem').[14]

Baxter's allegiance to the poem-producing 'gap' directly influ-
enced his writing; accounting in a major way for his tendency to be
formally derivative and thematically repetitive. For all his early
flourish and rhetorical extravagance, and despite the staggering
quantity of verse he produced – he averaged nearly two poems a
week for almost forty years – Baxter's only significant technical
innovation was the loose-unrhymed couplet form, modelled on
Lawrence Durrell, which he perfected in the late 1960s for the
Jerusalem Sonnets. While he was a masterful technician, innovation
wasn't his priority and he never deviated from his early belief that
a poet should have 'a basis of traditionalism and veneer of
modernism to give facility of expression and mood'.[15] He held an
enduring view on the importance of emotion, calling it 'the essence
of poetry, vowel-music promotes it, rhythm facilitates its flow'.[16]
The emotion influencing Baxter's idiom throughout his life surely
prompted Curnow's observation that he sought 'the eloquent rather
than the inquisitively precise word',[17] which, while accurate,
discounts the importance to Baxter of the emotionally precise.

Because poetry for Baxter was always a type of conversation, his
most successful poems took the form of verse letters. In these epis-
tolary poems his language seems most natural and colloquial, the
verse least structured and the ideas fresh off the top of the mind. It
is remarkable how exact and apt his use of language is, how care-
fully metaphor is used or extended, and how subtly a complex idea
can be expressed through the barest articulation of a concept or
experience. Often Baxter's poems are letters to himself, like entries
in a verse diary or the building blocks of a grand testamentary poem
carefully crafted to connect back and forward through metaphor and
imagery.

Baxter's 'gap' also explains why he was so often at odds with a
New Zealand society unable to stomach its disturbing reflection in

his work. His deficiencies have been extensively catalogued — perhaps most often and most honestly by him: he left a trail of broken friendships and relationships, his attitudes to women were problematic, his infidelities were legendary, his depictions of the middle classes were offensive to them, and his challenges to conventional morality were disturbing. But he also valued every experience, good or bad, for he classed as his most successful poems those containing a 'kernel of actual experiential knowledge',[18] and emphasised the intimate connection between his life experiences and his verse: 'I know only a little about the world; and most of it is somewhere in the poems I have written.'[19] However, when biographical elements occur in the poems they are generally projected through a mythic lens. He once described each of his poems as 'part of a large subconscious corpus of personal myth, like an island above the sea, but joined underwater to other islands',[20] and elsewhere commented that what 'happens is either meaningless to me, or else it is mythology'.[21] The elements Baxter the poet valued in his own and others' lives were those that connect individuals to a wider mythical landscape of human experience. In most of his verse there are no individuals, only archetypes like the 'National Mum and Labour Dad' of the 'Ballad of Calvary Street' (see p. 90).

One of Baxter's aims during the last years of his life was to present to other Pākehā (New Zealanders of European descent) an entirely new way of relating to Māori. This aim, reflected in both his life and his writing, was the outcome of a steadily intensifying identification, over a number of years, with Māori culture, tradition and spirituality. Through his marriage he had been drawn into participating in his wife's activities among her own Māori family. His efforts to understand the situation of Māori lie at the heart of poems like 'The Maori Jesus' (see p. 145) and 'Tangi' (see p. 173). The extent to which these efforts were successful is reflected in the fact that at his death he received the rare honour for a Pākehā of being buried in the urupā (graveyard) at Hiruharama following a full tangi (funeral rite) arranged by the elders of the local tribe, Ngāti Hau.

Towards the end of his life Baxter increasingly explored ways of putting into practice things he had been writing about. Impelled by recovery from alcoholism, conversion to Catholicism and a life-changing few months in Asia in the late 1950s, his conviction had grown that simply writing about his beliefs was insufficient.

Deprivation that was little more than theoretical in New Zealand was painfully real in India. At first he translated the concerns of his verse to a more externally dynamic medium by writing plays. Ultimately, his art and life coalesced in his move to found a commune at the isolated Māori settlement of Jerusalem. One feature of his decision to abandon his old life so ostentatiously was a commitment to stop writing poetry, an activity that now seemed at odds with a vocation of poverty. But he could no more stop writing than he could cease breathing. Instead of abandoning poetry he produced the *Jerusalem Sonnets*, perhaps his most significant and original epistolary sequence. Whereas earlier poems might, with formal metre and Latinate diction, move towards a final grand, sonorous phrase, now unrhymed run-on couplets (increasingly the unit of choice in his later work) create a tone both direct and personal, moving closer to a synthesis of Baxter's various selves that had for so long operated in tension. By resolving the conflicts in his personal mythmaking he effectively stepped from the local to the universal.

If, at times, Baxter appears to evaluate New Zealand society harshly, his judgements are always from the perspective of one intimately involved in the social process. His criticisms of national life and his ultimate decision to step out of the mainstream seemed to develop naturally from the preoccupations of a lifetime, which he repeatedly developed in his verse. Yet these preoccupations were, as a rule, neither negative nor despairing. Rather, the deliberately mythological cast of mind that underpinned his poetry sought to place the individual (and the nation) within a wider frame by directing attention towards universal elements of human experience. This is where James K. Baxter, the New Zealand poet, becomes truly a poet of the world. The man who found the Medusa's head of present-day urban global civilisation – with its 'depersonalisation, centralisation, [and] desacralisation' – intolerable, could still find reason for hope 'in the hearts of people'.[22]

Paul Millar
The University of Canterbury, New Zealand

Notes

1 H.D. McNaughton, 'Baxter, in Faulty Perspective', review of *James K. Baxter 1926–1972, A Memorial Volume*, ed. Alistair Taylor, *Christchurch Press*, 10 March 1973.

2 James K. Baxter, 'The Dragon Mask', in *Collected Poems*, ed. J.E. Weir (Wellington: Oxford University Press, 1995), p. 268.

3 'Shots Around the Target', *Chaff* XVIV.2 (September 1966), p. 1.

4 See 'He Waiata mo Te Kare', p. 230.

5 Allen Curnow, ed., Introduction, *A Book of New Zealand Verse: 1923–45* (Christchurch: Caxton Press, 1945), pp. 54–5.

6 Allen Curnow, ed., *The Penguin Book of New Zealand Verse* (Harmondsworth: Penguin Books, 1960) pp. 61, 62.

7 James K. Baxter, *The Man on the Horse* (Dunedin: University of Otago Press, 1967), p. 22. I am drawing in this paragraph on material prepared for a forthcoming book on Baxter's use of classical mythology, co-authored with Geoffrey Miles and John Davidson of Victoria University of Wellington.

8 *Ibid.*, p. 123.

9 *Ibid.*, p. 17.

10 *Ibid.*, p. 19.

11 James K. Baxter, interviewed on Radio New Zealand, *c.* 1963.

12 James K. Baxter, *Autumn Testament*, ed. Paul Millar (Auckland: Oxford University Press, 1997), p. 9.

13 *The Man on the Horse*, pp. 30–1.

14 This phenomenon in New Zealand culture has been examined in John Newton's innovative study *The Double Rainbow: James K. Baxter, Ngāti Hau and the Jerusalem Commune* (Wellington: Victoria University Press, 2009).

15 James K. Baxter, letter to Noel Ginn, *c.* July 1943, MS McKay 28/15.

16 James K. Baxter, letter to Noel Ginn, 6 November 1943, MS McKay 28/23.

17 Allen Curnow, ed., Introduction, *A Book of New Zealand Verse: 1923–45*, p. 55.

18 J.E. Weir, Introduction, *The Bone Chanter: Unpublished Poems 1945–72* by James K. Baxter (Wellington: Oxford University Press, 1976), p. 5.

19 James K. Baxter, 'The World of the Creative Artist', *Salient Literary Issue* (September 1955), p. 20.

20 James K. Baxter, *The Bone Chanter: Unpublished Poems 1945–72*, p. 6.

21 *The Man on the Horse*, p. 122.

22 James, K. Baxter, Introduction, *Notes on the Country I Live In* by Ans Westra (Wellington: A. Taylor, 1972), p. 8.

Note on the Text

This selection endeavours to give a sense of the broad range of Baxter's achievement, not merely its peaks, and thus it ranges from the comic and bawdy to the political and devotional. Apart from previously unpublished or uncollected poems, material in this volume corresponds as closely as possible to Baxter's *Collected Poems* edited by J.E. Weir. Previously published poems have two dates appended – the estimated year of composition in roman and the date of first publication in italics (a firm date is indicated by the addition of the day and month). Hitherto unpublished poems are followed by the Hocken Library, University of Otago manuscript reference number and approximate date of composition. In the rare case that Baxter did not give a poem a title, I have either followed Weir or supplied my own in square brackets.

Words in Māori

In the years since Baxter attempted to learn Māori, great efforts have been made to clarify and standardise pronunciation. This has particularly been the case with regard to long vowels, which are now indicated by a macron over the vowel where earlier, if they were indicated at all, it was by doubling the vowel (e.g. 'Maaori' for 'Māori'). I have chosen not to macronise any of Baxter's words in Māori (or to correct occasional small errors) when quoting directly, on the grounds that there is no evidence he always used correct pronunciation, and that the rhyme or rhythm of some poems might in fact depend on a more English-sounding pronunciation of the word. However, in the rest of the text I have endeavoured to use the correct macronised spelling. I have also spelled Whanganui River with an 'h', according to the 1991 convention established by local tribes, but have left it as 'Wanganui' in Baxter's text.

THE 1940S

Hocken Library, The University of Otago

James Keir Baxter was born in Dunedin in 1926; the second son of Archibald Baxter, an Otago farmer and notorious pacifist, and Millicent Baxter (née Brown). His middle name – after the Scottish socialist and pacifist, the first British Labour MP, Keir Hardie – signified his parents' left-leaning politics. Because of Baxter's stated tendency to mythologise his life in verse, biography is important in any study. His parents' socialist and pacifist beliefs profoundly influenced him, as did their strikingly contrasting backgrounds: Archie was a quiet, self-educated man, whose ancestors had been small farmers in the Scottish Highlands; and Millicent was the strong-minded eldest daughter of a noted Christchurch professor of English and Classics, John Macmillan Brown.

Apart from brief periods in Wanganui, England and Europe, Baxter grew up in Brighton, a small settlement on the Otago Coast south of Dunedin. A lifelong suspicion of education systems developed as he first attended Brighton Primary School and later Quaker schools in Wanganui and the English Cotswolds, and Dunedin's King's High School.

The early 1940s were not a good period for pacifists: the family was suspected of spying, James was bullied, and his older brother Terence sent into detention as a military defaulter. Adolescence was therefore a solitary time, but Baxter felt that his experiences 'created a gap in which the poems were able to grow'. Indeed, between 1942 and 1946 he would draft some 600 poems.

An able, although unmotivated, student, Baxter matriculated a year early, with unspectacular results, applying himself meanwhile to reading and emulating almost the entire English poetic canon. The moderns, particularly Auden, Spender, MacNeice and Day Lewis, inspired him with the voice they were giving to the social battles of the time. By his late teens he was developing a discernible voice out of adolescent imitation.

In 1944, Baxter began a 'long, unsuccessful love affair with the Higher Learning' when he enrolled at Otago University. 'Incipient alcoholism' soon became a problem, but in 1944 he also won the

Macmillan Brown literary prize (for 'Convoys') and Caxton Press published his first collection, *Beyond the Palisade*, to critical acclaim.

This remarkable debut volume is a selection of thirty-four poems from some 500 written between the ages of fifteen and eighteen. Allen Curnow selected six poems from it for his groundbreaking anthology *A Book of New Zealand Verse: 1923–45*, describing Baxter's poems as 'a new occurrence in New Zealand: strong in impulse and confident in invention, with qualities of youth in verse which we have lacked'. His endorsement established Baxter's reputation before many New Zealanders had read his work.

Critics commented on Baxter's style and tone, with its mix of imitation and assimilation of numerous major poets of the English canon – Yeats, Auden, MacNeice, Keats, Blake and Shelley, to name a few. No one, however, disagreed with Curnow's observation that Baxter had also written 'some poems which could only be his and only a New Zealander's'. Despite this, Baxter privately acknowledged a certain unevenness in the volume and described it as 'a sort of poet's progress'. A second collection, *Cold Spring*, considered by Baxter to be somewhat better than the first, remained unpublished.

Abandoning university study, from 1945 to 1947 Baxter worked in factories and on farms. Part of this period is fictionalised in his novel *Horse* (1985). His struggle with alcoholism was both cause and consequence of the failure of his first significant love affair, with a young medical student. Her enduring effect, however, is evident in three poem sequences: 'Songs of the Desert', 'Cressida' and 'Words to Lay a Strong Ghost'. An even more important relationship began in 1947 when he met Jacqueline (Jacquie) Sturm.

In late 1947 Baxter moved to Christchurch, ostensibly to renew his university studies, but actually to visit a Jungian psychologist. He began incorporating Jungian symbolism into his poetic theory and practice. His behaviour, thanks to the 'irrigating river of alcohol', could be erratic as he sporadically attended lectures and took jobs as a sanatorium porter, copy editor for the Christchurch *Press*, and in an abattoir. He began associating with the poets Curnow and Glover, and his reading remained copious.

Blow, Wind of Fruitfulness (1948) confirmed Baxter as the pre-eminent poet of his generation. Where *Beyond the Palisade* is occasionally uneven and too obviously imitative, and the unpublished *Cold Spring* dense with personal symbolism, the poems of *Blow, Wind of Fruitfulness* have more control and assurance. Curnow was moved to describe Baxter as 'the most original of New Zealand poets now living'. He argued that if 'these poems are full of echoes, they are not the echoes of mimicry but the true, if altered, accents of other voices, inherited by right of a natural eloquence'.

The New Zealand landscape plays an important role in the poems of *Blow, Wind of Fruitfulness*, as it did in *Beyond the Palisade*. Its spaces are again sparsely peopled and consequently a tone of solitude and alienation recurs. What is new is what Curnow called a 'welcome gain in irony and detachment'. The pompous and laboured 'University Song', for example, is delightfully subverted in an 'Envoi' in which the final lines encapsulate Baxter's reservations about 'the higher learning': '*Lost one original heart and mind* / Between the pub and the lecture room.'

Baxter's interest in religion led to baptism as an Anglican, and, despite considerable parental concern, he and Jacquie were married in St John's Cathedral, Napier, in 1948. That same year they moved to Wellington, where their daughter Hilary was born in 1949.

Beyond the Palisade

My soul as censer clear
    In a translucent breast
Shall burn, while dawn-clouds lower,
    With inner rest.

Beyond the palisade
    Shall I communion hold
Nor turn my steps aside
    For malice manifold.

The veil that sways unseen
    Above a frozen sea
Breaks to the spirit sane
    In multiplicity.

No law shall be obeyed
    No compass-guide save one
'Seek out thine own abode
    By solitary sun.'

Dim figures that I frame
    And on the night behold
Shall be writ large in flame
    Ere anarchy is old.

The full self-confidence
    May fall bereft from me
While in soul-mocking dance
    The splendid visions flee.

Yet shall I hold in all
    The faith that none may see –
The inmost citadel
    Of strong integrity.

1942 *1944*

The Mountains

In this scarred country, this cold threshold land,
The mountains crouch like tigers. By the sea
Folk talk of them hid vaguely out of sight.
But here they stand in massed solidity
To seize upon the day and night horizon.

Men shut within a whelming bowl of hills
Grow strange, say little when they leave their high
Yet buried homesteads. Return there silently
When thunder of night-rivers fills the sky
And giant wings brood over loftily and near.

The mountains crouch like tigers. Or they wait
As women wait. The mountains have no age.
But O the heart leaps to behold them loom!
A sense as of vast fate rings in the blood. No refuge,
No refuge is there from the flame that reaches

Among familiar things and makes them seem
Trivial, vain. O spirit walks on the peaks!
Eye glances across a gorge to further crags.
There is no desire. But the stream, but the avalanche speaks,
And their word is louder than freedom, the mountain embrace
Were a death dearer than freedom or freedom's flags.

I will go to the coastline and mingle with men.
These mountain buttresses build beyond the horizon.
They call. But he whom they lay their spell upon
Leaves home, leaves kindred. The range of the telescope's eye
Is well, if the brain follows not to the outermost fields of vision.
I shall drown myself in humanity. Better to lie
Dumb in the city than under the mountainous wavering sky.

The mountains crouch like tigers.
They are but stone yet the seeking eyes grow blind.

1942 *1944*

Love-Lyric III

The calm of summer burns, a steady flame.
            And a wolf-spider near me
prowls, his smooth
back like wood-splinters; on the sleek paint
of the verandah he
sways and pirouettes. I blow on
him, and he is still a moment.
            Flies flicker. A circular saw
droning, ringing, clanging
gashes the air with blades of sound:
and sensual the
awareness of new-cut saplings bitten
by bitter blades bitten.
            Gliding and
            fluttering
a butterfly crosses the
oval flower-plot;
iceland poppies
jostle beneath him
and seeded flowers ripen.
            The smoke-green wattle patterns
light and shade.
            The air like water murmurs
shaking small birch leaves:
the earth like fire responding;
and the sun moves over my hair
with sweaty fingers.
            A farm of corrugated iron roof
cuts the curve of grass dunes;
            metallic foliage against
the new-wrought ploughland.
Avalanche on avalanche
over it at
the scrub-hill horizon
baroque clouds billow
snow-crystal on the blue

snow-basilisk
snow-crystal on the blue
(the Venusberg to young Tannhäuser calling).
       The wolf-spider moves beside me
prey in his fangs.

6 March 1944 1944

Letter to Noel Ginn

They can admire the empty lion-skin
The heart skewered by print, who will admire:
But from you, Noel, I wish more –
The friend's stance, confessor for my sin
Which is pride alone: yet pride alone will win
Niche of immortal marble despised and hungered for.

       As a child I was childish … an intuitional ease;
Had missed the vice of sensitivity;
Waded the flood-race of a century;
But felt capacity for pain increase
Till each day no longer a wood of peace
Held larks of Shelleyan song, tigers of poetry.

       When I saw Europe … a kaleidoscope
Fluttered, flashed elusive in place of the grave
Time-wading fortitude: – oil-weighted wave
Feathering bows forever; blind seascape;
Nights of storm, screw thudding; Gibraltar cape –
Peered through field-glasses, played chess till nausea claimed her
                                                            slave.

       Or earlier: in Australia the hot days;
Mast-cracking Sydney bridge; golden Colombo
With fishing-fleets on estuaries to show
A bird's plumage, a bird's surf-shadowing ways;
A camel scrubbed upon the banks near Suez;
Crete's iron citadel; and Plymouth bitter with snow.

London claimed me: she was heavy and huge;
Her barges, and her dank wharves flecked with soot;
Placarded Tubes; and fog at Christmas; mute
Paling and palace. The Cotswolds were a refuge:
Leaf-mould ... stone ... thatched roofs ... blackberry hedge;
Lanes, willows ... snow-slush; bells; homesickness; running the
                                                    gauntlet.

Europe claimed me: then she did not bleed.
Flat Danish fields, yellow sky spun by the rocking
Express; and at Copenhagen seabirds flocking
Along quays. The rock Rhine towered and treed;
Clean Berlin; at Eisenach sycamore seed;
Rothenberg ... dungeons; friendly Storm Trooper ... the wind is
                                                    mocking.

France: where the Rhône ran under concrete;
Sewer at bridge-base. Out of the violent sun
I wrote poems, scrapped poems half-begun
On clouds and comets. A tower seen from the street:
Skeletons found there. Bats. Snake at my feet.
The castle ... Terry's arm broken; when set, he sweated with pain.

And Scotland was my spiritual home,
Or so it seemed. The tide ancestral swung
Over rock-weed. I plucked the bells of ling;
Saw bald Glencoe ... and watched the red-coats come.
Old Edinburgh ... were the cobbles dumb?
England again: Boscastle ... crags and a blowhole spouting.

– Here once more I walk in the troubled water.
Our hills call: but what shall I learn from them?
Pride bids me stare upon the broken time
Of lies and high explosive; prompts this letter.
With pride for armour men in their abattoir slaughter.
Pride holds me from like hells: pride makes me what I am.

What land shall receive me save as a stranger?
Sea-blown Ulysses said: and Ithaca
More alien was than Troy. Nor could Minerva
Content him long: aged he craved for danger
For withered fame. So Time was Troy's avenger.
Slight parallel ... yet seek I *res habita*.

The same inhuman cataclysm that set
You weeding flax upon a worthless ground
Both truth and talent to a treadmill bound
Leaves me upon a waiting Ararat:
(The flood may not subside): no marionette
Jerked by the city string, nor in her rubble drowned.

Both clouds and houses are a frozen tide
Till poetry inhabit them with fire.
Men only stay, their masque and their desire;
Thus among men I move my tap-roots wide
The roots of verse, the roots of life beside;
Leave empty lion-skin for dullards to admire.

Women as flowers: they are embodiment
Of the gross earth and the rhetorical cloud;
But shaped as bird, as flower to strange and loud.
... A span of threescore and the heart is spent:
This word invades, but I have armament –
The gift of ancestry, the armour of the proud.

The backward groping of a tree of blood
Coils in the dark: but from its mountain springs
Brings mountain pride, and brings
Each impulse of the evil and the good,
With something of a Celtic hardihood:
The pain and poetry ... I did not dream these things.

Those who grew old: those who were shrewd and hardy;
As children wondered and as men grew sure:
They are but painted figures insecure
Upon a tattered backcloth tamed and tardy.
And we their unreflecting progeny
Forget, inherit: thus their deeds, their deaths endure.

My son, at first a knocking in the womb
Can speak beyond the thundering gates of war,
Symplegades: it is his voice I hear;
And my son's son; braving the storms of time
The storms and sultry shallows – vortex, storm,
They beat on us, they break: pride is the saviour.

1944 *1944*

The First Forgotten

O fons Bandusiae!
The green hill-orchard where
My great-granduncle lived
Is overgrown. No cache and no reprieve

The chilly air holds. They came from the
Old lands, for hunger, or fearing the young
Would shoot from thicket a keeper,
Be transported or hung.

So beholding the strange reeds,
Arrogant flax and fen,
They saw release, eventual and ancestral peace,
Building the stubborn clans again:

Beehives along an elderberry fence …
The land is drained. Gorse
Only will grow. To the towns now
Their sons' sons gone, expanding universe:

A light and brittle birth.
I would glorify
Innumerable men in whose breasts my heart once beat,
Is beating. They were slow to die.

One who drove a bullock team
In the gold-rush on an upland track.
One smiling and whistling softly
With a horseshoe behind his back.

Steel mutilates: more, the hollow
Facade, the gaudy mask
On a twisted face. Clay-shut, forgetful, shall
They answer? we ask?

Only the rough and paper bark peeling
From young bluegums, while undergrowth
Among stunted apple-trees coiling
Trips the foot. Sods grass-buried like antique faith.

1944 1944

University Song

Among these hills our fathers came.
By strength of eye and hand alone
They built: and murmur loud as flame
Their voices from the living stone.

Forget not those whom Scotland bred
Above whose bones our cities stand.
Forget not them! nor the unknown dead
Whose broken veins flow through our land.

As streams in wildernesses rise
And green the desolate shingle plain:
So under windy southern skies
Peace flowered and Wisdom shall remain.

The generations rouse and pass
Like falling birds to well of night,
Or like the windsown summer grass
Now tall, now withered in our sight.

But our sons' sons alike shall find
Perpetual, though nations cease,
Within these walls the quiet mind
The storm-unshaken rose of Peace.

1945 *1948*

Envoi [to 'University Song']

And blackened by the early frost
Leaves beat upon the window pane
Like paper mouths – an image lost
Between the eyeball and the brain.

Above, about, on either hand
Their multitudinous seven wings
The uncreated winds expand
In sufferance of created things.

Where evening darkening in dejection
Can hear, monotonous, profound
The too long dead for resurrection
In suspiration from the ground –

Attenuate ghosts expound their lean
Philosophies of When and If;
And oft on that enchanted green
Chimera mates with hippogriff.

The classics student feels an urge
To emulate Empedocles
But rides upon the lava surge –
Oh forest of the bloody trees –

Per ardua ad astra: blind
Inscription from a catacomb.
Lost, one original heart and mind
Between the pub and lecture-room.

1946 *1948*

High Country Weather

Alone we are born
      And die alone;
Yet see the red-gold cirrus
      Over snow-mountain shine.

Upon the upland road
      Ride easy, stranger:
Surrender to the sky
      Your heart of anger.

4 October 1945 *1948*

Blow, Wind of Fruitfulness

Blow, wind of fruitfulness
    Blow from the buried sun:
Blow from the buried kingdom
    Where heart and mind are one.

Blow, wind of fruitfulness,
    The murmuring leaves remember;
For deep in doorless rock
    Awaits their green September.

Blow from the wells of night:
    The blind flower breathes thy coming
Birds that are silent now
    And buds of barren springing.

Blow from beyond our day.
    The hill-born streams complain;
Hear from their stony courses
    The great sea rise again.

Blow on the mouth of morning
    Renew the single eye:
And from remembered darkness
    Our immortality.

19 January 1946 1948

Odysseus

Blaze I saw once beyond a barren coast
Live tropic seas and continents of love
But not now so: my ready heart was lost
Between the trough and crest of the climbing wave.
For ringing Troy was cold – though I donned death
And wily rode the anarchic battle there,
Tricked brutish heroes into fear beneath
An iron thought, blunting the brazen spear.
Troy died in me long ere her ashes died;
On shore or alien quicksand or drowned deep
In deepsea night, my death-born brethren hide
Their trusting eyes. What though Calypso weep
Or blind Penelope, trees guessing not the snow –
Death is more deep than love: death is my spirit now.

1946 *1948*

Returned Soldier

The boy who volunteered at seventeen
At twenty-three is heavy on the booze.
Strafed in the desert and bombed out in Crete –
With sore dark eyes and hardened by the heat
Entitled now to call himself a man
And in the doll's-house walk with death at ease:
The Cairo women, cobbers under sand
A death too great for dolls to understand.

Back to a city bed or station hut
At maelstrom centre falling through the night
To dreams where deeper than El Alamein
A buried childhood stirs with leaves and flowers
Remembered girls, the blurred and bitter waters.
Wakes to the midnight rafters and the rain.

1946 *1948*

The Bay

On the road to the bay was a lake of rushes
Where we bathed at times and changed in the bamboos.
Now it is rather to stand and say:
How many roads we take that lead to Nowhere,
The alley overgrown, no meaning now but loss:
Not that veritable garden where everything comes easy.

And by the bay itself were cliffs with carved names
And a hut on the shore beside the Maori ovens.
We raced boats from the banks of the pumice creek
Or swam in those autumnal shallows
Growing cold in amber water, riding the logs
Upstream, and waiting for the taniwha.

So now I remember the bay and the little spiders
On driftwood, so poisonous and quick.
The carved cliffs and the great outcrying surf
With currents round the rocks and the birds rising.
A thousand times an hour is torn across
And burned for the sake of going on living.
But I remember the bay that never was
And stand like stone, and cannot turn away.

1946 *1948*

Sea Noon

The grey smoke of rain drifts over headlands
And clear drops fall on the paper as I write.
Only the light thunder and murmur
Of ebbing and flowing furrows is endlessly repeated
And the rapid gulls flash over without sound.

Where is a house with windows open to the afternoon?
With light beer on tables and tobacco smoke
Floating; with a fire in the grate;
With music and the mind-filling pleasure of easy company.
Lying back in a chair to laugh or standing and smiling
One would accept all fates, and even the gold
Melancholy leaves of late autumn
Would seem as natural as a child's toy.

But labour and hunger strides the year
In seasonal repetition, more harsh than tidal waters.
The very rocks are cold: and they were lava once.

So stand the dull green trees bearing the weather
On solitary boughs; so the grey smoke of rain
Drifts on a painted verge of sea and air.
The fisherman casts his net to hold the tide.
Chilly the light wind blowing. And dark the face of noonday
As at the inconsolable parting of friends.

10 June 1946 *1948*

Let Time be Still

Let Time be still
Who takes all things,
Face, feature, memory
Under his blinding wings.

That I hold again the green
Larch of your body
Whose leaves will gather
The springs of the sky.

And fallen from his cloud
The falcon find
The thigh-encompassed wound
Breasts silken under hand.

Though in a dark room
We knew the day breaking
And the rain-bearing wind
Cold matins making.

Sure it seemed
That hidden away
From the sorrowful wind
In deep bracken I lay.

Your mouth was the sun
And green earth under
The rose of your body flowering
Asking and tender
In the timelost season
Of perpetual summer.

1946 *1948*

Tunnel Beach

The waist-high sea was rolling
Thunder along her seven iron beaches
As we climbed down to rocks and the curved sand,
Drowned Lyonesse lay lost and tolling
Waiting the cry of the sun's phoenix
From the sea-carved cliffs that held us in their hand.

Forgotten there the green
Paddocks we walked an hour before,
The mare and the foal and the witch-tormented wood
And the flaked salt boughs, for the boughs of flame were seen
Of the first garden and the root
Of graves in your salt mouth and the forehead branded fire.

Through the rock tunnel whined
The wind, Time's hound in leash,
And stirred the sand and murmured in your hair.
The honey of your moving thighs
Drew down the cirrus sky, your doves about the beach
Shut out sea thunder with their wings and stilled the lonely air.

But O rising I heard the loud
Voice of the sea's women riding
All storm to come. No virgin mother bore
My heart wave eaten. From the womb of cloud
Falls now no dove, but combers grinding
Break sullen on the last inviolate shore.

1946 *1948*

Songs of the Desert, 8

As we have sown the changing breeze
And squandered our hearts' charity
For us no Theban Hercules
Can raise again the fallen sky,
Nor shall the great angelic throng
That trembled at an infant's cry
Echo anew our broken song.

So if memorial is meant
Lie it must in my weak word.
Fruit of the casual sacrament
That burns likewise for beast and bird,
Go then, brief candle, tell to man
How once our inland waters heard
The rumour of Leviathan.

O when I remember how
Breast to breast we have lain
In earth's compassionate afterglow,
The fallen tower is reared again:
Heart as blind as a darkened room
And our every act a vain
Hieroglyph in a desert tomb.

1947 *1957*

To my Father

Today, looking at the flowering peach,
The island off the shore and waves that break
Quiet upon the rocks and level beach –
We must join forces, you and I, remake
The harbour silted and the city bombed
And all our hopes that lie now fire-entombed.

Your country childhood helped to make you strong,
Ploughing at twelve. I only know the man.
While I grew up more sheltered and too long
In love with my disease; though illness can
Impart by dint of pain a different kind
Of toughness to the predatory mind.

There is a feud between us. I have loved
You more than my own good, because you stand
For country pride and gentleness, engraved
In forehead lines, veins swollen on the hand;
Also, behind slow speech and quiet eye
The rock of passionate integrity.

You were a poet whom the time betrayed
To action. So, as Jewish Solomon
Prayed for wisdom, you had prayed
That you might have a poet for a son.
The prayer was answered; but an answer may
Confound by its exactness those who pray.

Finding no fault in you, I have been tempted
To stay your child. But that which broke
(Nature) the navel-cord, has not exempted
Even your light and sympathetic yoke.
It is in me your own true mettle shows;
Nor can we thus be friends till we are foes.

This you know well, but it will bear repeating –
Almost you are at times a second self;

Almost at times I feel your heart beating
In my own breast as if there were no gulf
To sever us. And you have seemed then rather
An out-of-time twin brother than a father.

So much is true; yet I have seen the time
When I would cut the past out, like a cancer,
Which now I must digest in awkward rhyme
Until I move 'in measure like a dancer'.
To know an age where all our loves have scope:
It is too much for any man to hope.

You, tickling trout once in a water-race;
You, playing cards, not caring if you lost;
You, shooting hares high on the mountain face;
You, showing me the ferns that grow from frost;
You, quoting Burns and Byron while I listened;
You, breaking quartz until the mica glistened.

These I remember, with the wind that blows
Forever pure down from the tussock ranges;
And these remain, like the everlasting snows,
Changeless in me while my life changes;
These, and a thousand things that prove
You rooted like a tree in the land's love.

I shall compare you to the bended bow,
Myself the arrow launched upon the hollow
Resounding air. And I must go
In time, my friend, to where you cannot follow.
It is not love would hope to keep me young,
The arrow rusted and the bow unstrung.

We have one aim: to set men free
From fear and custom and the incessant war
Of self with self and city against city –
So they may know the peace that they were born for
And find the earth sufficient, who instead
For fruit give scorpions and stones for bread.

And I sit now beside the wishing-well
And drop my silver down. I will have sons
And you grandchildren yet to tell
Old tales despite the anger of the guns:
Leisure to stroll and see Him unafraid
Who walked with Adam once in the green shade.

1947 *1953*

The Cave

In a hollow of the fields, where one would least expect it,
Stark and suddenly this limestone buttress:
A tree whose roots are bound about the stones,
Broad-leaved, hides well that crevice at the base
That leads, one guesses, to the sunless kingdom
Where souls endure the ache of Proserpine.

Entering where no man it seemed
Had come before, I found a rivulet
Beyond the rock door running in the dark.
Where it sprang from in the heart of the hill
No one could tell: alone
It ran like Time there in the dank silence.

I spoke once and my voice resounded
Among the many pillars. Further in
Were bones of sheep that strayed and died
In nether darkness, brown and water-worn.
The smell of earth was like a secret language
That dead men speak and we have long forgotten.

The whole weight of the hill hung over me;
Gladly I would have stayed there and been hidden
From every beast that moves beneath the sun,
From age's enmity and love's contagion:
But turned and climbed back to the barrier,
Pressed through and came to dazzling daylight out.

1948 *1948*

Farmhand

You will see him light a cigarette
At the hall door careless, leaning his back
Against the wall, or telling some new joke
To a friend, or looking out into the secret night.

But always his eyes turn
To the dance floor and the girls drifting like flowers
Before the music that tears
Slowly in his mind an old wound open.

His red sunburnt face and hairy hands
Were not made for dancing or love-making
But rather the earth wave breaking
To the plough, and crops slow-growing as his mind.

He has no girl to run her fingers through
His sandy hair, and giggle at his side
When Sunday couples walk. Instead
He has his awkward hopes, his envious dreams to yarn to.

But ah in harvest watch him
Forking stooks, effortless and strong –
Or listening like a lover to the song
Clear, without fault, of a new tractor engine.

1948 *1948*

Letter to Noel Ginn II

Two years of silence – I take pen again
To write a rhyming letter. You'll forgive
The interim, and knowing how we live
From hand to mouth, a certain thread of pain
And bitterness that blurs the narrative.
My last was in a more romantic vein.

Our dreams take refuge from the men we are
And hide as flies do from the winter chill.
The lost traveller's dream under the hill
Remains with me when propping up a bar
Or in strange beds I do the body ill
To gratify a merciless guiding star.

'Th' expense of spirit ...' Yet the spirit grows
By grieving for the sensual heart in chains.
Birth-pangs that we mistake for burial-pains
Give promise of the everlasting rose
Where bitter Loss consolidates its gains.
This is the answer that no question knows.

I have the letters that you wrote from camp
(Defaulters' camp, in case this should be read
By other men) where living men grew dead
In grey monotony. I was a lamp,
A kind of beacon to you then, you said –
Since then the wick has grown a trifle damp.

No man can play Aladdin all his life.
The oil is blood, although the flame be clear,
And world-annihilating djinns appear
Unasked-for at the falling of a leaf.
Or else the heart becomes a cinder – Fear
Is Art's companion, and the hermit Grief.

So poets learn to live like other men
For money, lovers, or the friends with whom
Music can animate a sunless room
And rouse the rumour of a different Sun
That shines the same though endless night draw on
And wakes the dead heart from its numbered tomb.

Perhaps I overstate the case — but I
Live by extremes. The madman and the saint
Have both (I fear) the same extremist taint,
And both are mad to Madame Butterfly.
Being no Francis, I can scarcely paint
A halo — 'poet's licence' is my cry.

It was my dearly held delusion once
That labouring men were better than their betters
And needed only to throw off their fetters
For Eden to return to Adam's sons.
Since then I've worked with them; and they're go-getters
Just like the Rev. Fraser — bless his bones.

An 8 hour day is not conducive to
The exercise of one's imagination.
So I have found alas that my true station
Is still among the academic crew
Whom I despised for undue cerebration
That leads to withering of the heart and thew.

No doubt I'll find a niche where I can grumble
About the clique that pay me for my pen,
And drink with other intellectual men,
And gain some slight prestige, however humble,
With a little bitter poem now and then
Until the first apocalyptic rumble:

And that will be the Bomb. I often think
Of the climb we made like beetles up a drain
From neanderthal, to be washed down again
In a flood of dirty water from the sink.
Lions and horses also sport a brain
But do not pine for a celestial stink.

From this high window I can see the swells
Roll in with their incessant cannonade
Upon that shore where once, a lonely child, I made
My own mythology of weeds and shells
And dreamed I heard from the green water shade
The pealing of sea drowned cathedral bells.

(While in bombed Germany the violent dream
Grew flesh and blood and tore a city down
Whose dazed survivors searching among stones
Can find the lichen hunger or the scream
Of mandrake pain, but never that first sun-
Flower of peace upon a lucid stream.)

And it is good to walk upon the sand
In winter when the dunes are hard and dry
With frost that binds an iron earth and sky.
Bone of my bone, the stubborn rocks withstand
The ebb and surge of grief. The ocean I
Once feared, I love more than the frozen land.

There is a kind of reconciliation
With buried selves and seasons, so to walk
And listen to the arrogant seabirds' talk
Who have no interest in our damnation,
And feel beyond those frosty hillocks the
Thunder of an obliterating sea.

14 April 1946–8 *1948*

Poem by the Clock Tower, Sumner

Beside the dark sand and the winged foam
Under the shadow of the naked tower
Play the wild children, stranger than Atlanteans.
For them the blazed rock hieroglyph burns clear:
Bear dance and bull dance in the drenched arena
To the sun's trumpet and the waves' crying.

They are the terrible mirrors where our time
Stares back with gorgon eyes. An Ice Age lies
Between us; for they know
The place and hour of the young phoenix' nest
On the bare dune where we can see only
Worn glacial stones and terminal moraine.

And for them rises yet
From earth's still centre the heaven-bearing
Immortal Tree. The ponds and hollow groves
Peopled with fish and speaking birds receive them,
Teach them the language in which stones converse,
Show them the arrows of the toi-toi plume.

We in the murdering city hug our death
Closer than jewels; to the mud-stained sky
Daylong expectant turn one questioning face.
Or in the long night frozen the caress
Of flesh on flesh and stone on stone are one
Suspending rainbow in the lost abyss.

Where is the white stone that shall transmute
Our average day to gold?
The green lane that leads to the wishing well
The secret house the fertile wilderness
Where grief and memory are reconciled.
Angels of fire and ice guard well that garden.

And yet the tower stands, four-square and casting
A sundial shadow on the dancing sand.
The blown cloud blares with trumpets. And the wind
Beyond the Cave Rock scatters birds and spume,
Strikes out an echo from the ringing stone,
Strikes where the boat is tugging at its chain.

These images disturb our human night
With joy, and promise of prodigious noon:
Childhoods and age in one green cradle joined.
Again from this blind rock of time I know
In heart of lethargy a drowned sun rising;
Again the dark Dove nestles in my breast.

1948 *1953*

Virginia Lake

The lake lies blind and glinting in the sun.
Among the reeds the red-billed native birds
Step high like dancers. I have found
A tongue to praise them, who was dumb,
And from the deaf morass one word
Breaks with the voices of the numberless drowned.

This was the garden and the talking water
Where once a child walked and wondered
At the leaves' treasure house, the brown ducks riding
Over the water face, the four winds calling
His name aloud, and a green world under
Where fish like stars in a fallen heaven glided.

And for his love the eyeless statues moved
Down the shell paths. The bandstand set
On fire with music blazing at its centre
Was havened in his love.
The lichened elm was rafters overhead,
Old waves unlocked their gates for him to enter.

Who now lies dumb, the black tongue dry
And the eyes weighed with coins.
O out of this rock tomb
Of labyrinthine grief, I start and cry
Toward his real day – the undestroyed
Fantastic Eden of a waking dream.

1947–8 *1953*

Hart Crane

This poet, fallen in love with a steel robot,
Drinking bad whisky in New York for years,
Wrung out catharsis in a urinal
And public poetry from private fears.

So pity him, that mining the black gold
Of prophecy, he dug his own grave.
Marshfire by night and at full noon the cold
Vertiginous terror of the buried alive.

And praise him who for the new Birdman built
That rainbow bridge which only gods can walk
(Forgetting the dark river underneath
Whose waves roll back a drunken sailor's talk).

Till Death, death, death, the black bells told
From towers of agony. Perfection was his vice:
And no man came where his heart glittered perfect
The violent crystal in a world of ice.

Till in the Caribbean that gross hulk
Face downward tossed in a widening wake, was free.
And his dead heart became a continent;
His hands unclenched embraced the swollen sea.

1948 *1948*

Wellington

Time is a frown on the stone brow
Of a monument, a gale shaking the quay.
There is never time to let the whole day sink
Into the heart, and hold it sheltered there.

Power breeds on power in labyrinthine hives
Nested under the daylong driving cloud;
Stale breath of suburb dawn hazing the harbour,
Tiring the eye, stripping the nerve to fever.

City of flower-plots, canyon streets and trams,
O sterile whore of a thousand bureaucrats!
There is a chasm of sadness behind
Your formal giggle, when the moon opens

Cold doors in space. Here on the dark hill
Above your broken lights – no crucifix
Entreats, but the gun emplacements overgrown
And the radio masts' huge harp of the wind's grief.

1949 *1953*

Rocket Show

As warm north rain breaks over suburb houses,
Streaming on window glass, its drifting hazes
Covering harbour ranges with a dense hood:
I recall how eighteen months ago I stood
Ankle-deep in sand on an Otago beach
Watching the fireworks flare over strident surf and bach,
In brain grey ash, in heart the sea-change flowing
Of one love dying and another growing.

For love grows like the crocus bulb in winter
Hiding from snow and from itself the tender
Green frond in embryo; but dies as rockets die
(White sparks of pain against a steel-dark sky)
With firebird wings trailing an arc of grief
Across a night inhuman as the grave,
Falling at length a dull and smouldering shell
To frozen dunes and the wash of the quenching swell.

There was little room left where the crowd had trampled
Grass and lupin bare, under the pines that trembled
In gusts from the sea. On a sandhillock I chose
A place to watch from. Then the rockets rose,
O marvellous, like self-destroying flowers
On slender stems, with seed-pods full of flares,
Raining down amber, scarlet, pennies from heaven
On the skyward straining heads and still sea-haven.
Had they brought death, we would have stood the same
I think, in ecstasy at the world-end flame.

It is the rain streaming reminds me of
Those ardent showers, cathartic love and grief.
As I walked home through the cold streets by moonlight,
My steps ringing in the October night,
I thought of our strange lives, the grinding cycle
Of death and renewal come to full circle,
And of man's heart, that blind Rosetta stone,
Mad as the polar moon, decipherable by none.

1949 *1953*

Wild Bees

Often in summer, on a tarred bridge plank standing,
Or downstream between willows, a safe Ophelia drifting
In a rented boat – I had seen them come and go,
Those wild bees swift as tigers, their gauze wings a-glitter
In passionless industry, clustering black at the crevice
Of a rotten cabbage tree, where their hive was hidden low.

But never strolled too near. Till one half-cloudy evening
Of ripe January, my friends and I
Came, gloved and masked to the eyes like plundering desperadoes,
To smoke them out. Quiet beside the stagnant river
We trod wet grasses down, hearing the crickets chitter
And waiting for light to drain from the wounded sky.

Before we reached the hive their sentries saw us
And sprang invisible through the darkening air,
Stabbed, and died in stinging. The hive woke. Poisonous fuming
Of sulphur filled the hollow trunk, and crawling
Blue flame sputtered – yet still their suicidal
Live raiders dived and clung to our hands and hair.

O it was Carthage under the Roman torches,
Or loud with flames and falling timber, Troy!
A job well botched. Half of the honey melted
And half the rest young grubs. Through earth-black smouldering ashes
And maimed bees groaning, we drew out our plunder.
Little enough their gold, and slight our joy.

Fallen then the city of instinctive wisdom.
Tragedy is written distinct and small:
A hive burned on a cool night in summer.
But loss is a precious stone to me, a nectar
Distilled in time, preaching the truth of winter
To the fallen heart that does not cease to fall.

1941–9 *1953*

Poem in the Matukituki Valley

Some few yards from the hut the standing beeches
Let fall their dead limbs, overgrown
With feathered moss and filigree of bracken.
The rotted wood splits clean and hard
Close-grained to the driven axe, with sound of water
Sibilant falling and high nested birds.

In winter blind with snow; but in full summer
The forest blanket sheds its cloudy pollen
And cloaks a range in undevouring fire.
Remote the land's heart. Though the wild scrub cattle
Acclimatized, may learn
Shreds of her purpose, or the taloned kea.

For those who come as I do, half-aware,
Wading the swollen
Matukituki waist-high in snow water,
And stumbling where the mountains throw their dice
Of boulders huge as houses, or the smoking
Cataract flings its arrows on our path –

For us the land is matrix and destroyer
Resentful, darkly known
By sunset omens, low words heard in branches;
Or where the red deer lift their innocent heads
Snuffing the wind for danger,
And from our footfall's menace bound in terror.

Three emblems of the heart I carry folded
For charms against flood water, sliding shale:
Pale gentian, lily, and bush orchid.
The peaks too have names to suit their whiteness,
Stargazer and Moonraker,
A sailor's language and a mountaineer's.

And those who sleep in close bags fitfully
Besieged by wind in a snowline bivouac –
The carrion parrot with red underwing
Clangs on the roof by night, and daybreak brings
Raincloud on purple ranges, light reflected
Stainless from crumbling glacier, dazzling snow.

Do they not, clay in that unearthly furnace,
Endure the hermit's peace
And mindless ecstasy? Blue-lipped crevasse
And smooth rock chimney straddling – a communion
With what eludes our net – Leviathan
Stirring to ocean birth our inland waters?

Sky's purity; the altar cloth of snow
On deathly summits laid; or avalanche
That shakes the rough moraine with giant laughter;
Snowplume and whirlwind – what are these
But His flawed mirror who gave the mountain strength
And dwells in holy calm, undying freshness?

Therefore we turn, hiding our souls' dullness
From that too blinding glass: turn to the gentle
Dark of the human daydream, child and wife,
Patience of stone and soil, the lawful city
Where man may live, and no wild trespass
Of what's eternal shake his grave of time.

1949 *1953*

THE 1950S

Private collection

In 1950, following the move to Wellington with his new family, Baxter enrolled at Victoria University College. He also began associating with a generation of writers – among them W.H. Oliver, Alistair Campbell and Louis Johnson – who would become known as the Wellington Group.

In 1951, now attending Wellington Teachers' College, Baxter enthralled the New Zealand Writers' Conference with his lecture *Recent Trends in New Zealand Poetry*, subsequently published by Caxton Press. One reviewer described him as 'the profoundest critic we have'. A selection of poems in a collaborative volume, *Poems Unpleasant*, was published in 1952.

Having completed his Teachers' College course, Baxter studied full-time at Victoria University in 1953, also publishing *The Fallen House*, a collection that exhibited greater confidence and maturity through the evenness of its tone and the less emphatic echoes of Baxter's many adolescent influences. A few poems exhibit an uncharacteristic simplicity more common in later collections. But usually, when Baxter writes about natural features or everyday events, he develops his themes to communicate a hidden meaning, or connect images of the landscape to the wider landscapes of human experience.

In 1954 he was assistant master at Lower Hutt's Epuni School. An able teacher, but no disciplinarian, his major contribution was a series of children's poems published posthumously in 1974 as *The Tree House*. Also in 1954, he gave three Macmillan Brown lectures on poetry at Victoria University, published – to mixed reviews from critics concerned by his simplification of issues and reliance upon anecdote – as *The Fire and the Anvil* (1955).

In late 1954, Baxter joined Alcoholics Anonymous, espousing its principle of helping others in a course of counselling and prison visitation that continued for the rest of his life. Greater stability – personal, financial and domestic – was also achieved through a substantial legacy with which the family purchased a house in the Wellington suburb of Ngaio. He received his BA in 1955 and published a long poem in pamphlet form, *Traveller's Litany*. He left Epuni School in 1956 to work for the School Publications section of the Department of Education, a period which provided material for numerous attacks on bureaucracy.

Baxter discovered the pitfalls of parody when his skilful imitations of seventeen New Zealand poets, *The Iron Breadboard: Studies in New Zealand Writing* (1957), was received with acrimony by some of his peers. Fourteen more serious poems appeared in a collaboration, *The Nightshift: Poems on Aspects of Love* (1957), a collection that, to quote Howard McNaughton, 'established a position of alienation that would recur in his work for two decades'. The following year Baxter received international recognition when Oxford University Press published *In Fires of No Return*. Despite this recognition and the book's selection as the Poetry Book Society's Choice, the collection, which is divided into three sections, was not judged successful by critics. Section one, some stronger early poems, and section two, a number of previously uncollected pieces, received little criticism. However section three, Baxter's more recent work, was censured for its many poems that contain superb lines or phrases yet fail to achieve wholeness.

Baxter's greatest success in 1958 was his radio play, broadcast in September, *Jack Winter's Dream*. Domestically, things were less successful. Jacquie was astonished by Baxter's unheralded decision to convert to Roman Catholicism and in October 1957 they separated. He was received into the Church in 1958.

A UNESCO Fellowship to study educational publishing in Japan and India gave Baxter and Jacquie a chance to reconcile. He left for Japan in September 1958 and the family joined him later in India. Baxter was overwhelmed by the poverty and the situation of ethnic minorities. The Indian poor would haunt his imagination and his poetry.

Returning to New Zealand wasted by dysentery, he showed increasing disillusionment with New Zealand society. Drama became a vehicle for such criticism. *The Wide Open Cage*, which was staged in 1959 by Richard Campion, explored themes such as guilt and alienation in relationships.

A Rented Room

Surprisingly he woke to a daylight room
For once not hostile – lay inertly, feeling
Close walls maternal fold chair, bed, and flax mat in
As if they bounded rather a womb or tomb;
Explored the plaster countries on the ceiling
And the rough touch of the blanket on his naked skin –

Delighting him, who for the moment had
Money, a mistress, all that the young require
To walk Niagara: so, whistle and shunting
Of trains in early fog, the beery glad
Eye of a newmade sun, promised a durable fire
And fleshly peace in a room's nest no more found wanting.

It was shelter, bourne, beginning, but no cage,
His own place. Indeed he seemed to lie
Masterless at length at the good centre
Of nineteen years' maze, the green boy come of age –
Not seeing the handsized cloud in the clear sky
And the door ajar to let the Furies enter.

1950 *1953*

The Fallen House

I took the clay track leading
From Black Bridge to Duffy's farm,
In no forefarer's footmark treading,
Thus free, it would seem, from any harm
That could befall me – the kind of ill-luck charm
That clings to a once-fair steading –

When South the sky thickened
And rain came pelter on the hill-scurf:
So in a grove (where the wind quickened
Their young leaves like the mile-off surf)
Of gums I sheltered, whose roots had drained the turf
Of life till a starved soil sickened.

But an older grief spoke plainly
From the green mound where thistle strewed
Her bearded gossamer. Ungainly
The sprawled stones fireblackened could
Recall man; though where the house stood
Stands ragged thistle only.

It was not Woe that flaunted
Funereal plume and banner there,
Nor an Atridean doom that daunted
The heart with a lidless gorgon stare;
But darker the cradling bluegums, sombre the air,
By the wraith of dead joy haunted.

There once the murk was cloven
By hearthlight fondly flaring within:
Adamant seemed their hope and haven.
O Time, Time takes in a gin
The quick of being! Pale now and gossamer-thin
The web their lives had woven.

1950 *1953*

Cressida, 11: Her Decision

Show me the face, cold mirror, that the world
Can see and prize: myself you'll never show.
Eyes wide apart, forehead a trifle low,
Rose-ruddy cheeks, the ripe mouth cupid-curled.
Blonde hair, they say, is fickle: I'm a blonde.
Then I'll stay home and read a book tonight;
Let him tire waiting, walk the lawn in spite.
They say, Fidelity's a standing pond
(But I'll not listen). How the mean thoughts swarm
Like flies in sunlight, sparks behind a grate!
It was not so: too much alone of late
I grow unsure. The waste wind blowing warm
Can ruffle the deep well of happiness
But never dry it. Oh the moon controls
Our sex, the subtle mercury our souls!
– The amber necklace then, and the grey dress.

1951 *1976*

The Bad Young Man

'Oh summer is a beggar's feast,'
      Cried the rumbustious bad young man,
'And Nobodaddy cares in the least
If we two make the two-backed beast —
So lie you down, lie you down!'
'I think my maiden aunt would frown,'
      She said under the yellow lupin.

'Gulls are tumbling on the wing,'
      Cried the rumbustious bad young man,
'And the little fishes have their fling:
So why should a scruple keep us waiting?
And O my dear, I love you so.'
'You'll tell a different tale tomorrow,'
      She said under the yellow lupin.

'O cover me with your tent of hair,'
      Groaned the rumbustious bad young man.
'Milk and honey, your breasts are bare,
My sucking dove, my silken mare —
Wherever you learnt it you have the knack.'
'Gentlier, or you'll break my back,'
      She moaned under the yellow lupin.

'Ah Love's joy was not made to last,'
      Sighed the rumbustious sad young man.
'The world's mill is grinding fast
And the sky, the sky is overcast —
But still, I thank you for your kindness.'
'I fear the sand has soiled my dress,'
      She said under the yellow lupin.

1951 *1958*

The Homecoming

Odysseus has come home, to the gully farm
Where the macrocarpa windbreak shields a house
Heavy with time's reliques – the brown-filmed photographs
Of ghosts more real than he; the mankind-measuring arm
Of a pendulum clock; and true yet to her vows,
His mother, grief's Penelope. At the blind the sea wind laughs.

The siege more long and terrible than Troy's
Begins again. A Love demanding all,
Hypochondriacal, seadark and contentless:
This was the sour ground that nurtured a boy's
Dream of freedom: this, in Circe's hall
Drugged him; his homecoming finds this, more relentless.

She does not say 'You have changed'; nor could she imagine any
Otherwise to the quiet maelstrom spinning
In the circle of their days. Still she would wish to carry
Him folded within her, shut from the wild and many
Voices of life's combat, in the cage of beginning;
She counts it natural that he should never marry.

She will cook his meals; complain of the south weather
That wrings her joints. And he – rebels; and yields
To the old covenant – calms the bleating
Ewe in birth travail. The smell of saddle leather
His sacrament; or the sale day drink; yet hears beyond sparse fields
On reef and cave the sea's hexameter beating.

1952 *1952*

Never No More

Oh the summer's afloat on spindrift beaches
Brown as bread in a holiday heaven:
The same sweet lie the lupin teaches
As always dropping her gay pollen
On a girl's print frock leg shoulder bare
Never no more never no more.

The boys climb to their branch-high houses
Under a black bridge dive for pennies
The noon cloud like a bird's breast downy
Night come cool as a hawthorn berry
Kite tails tied on a telephone wire
Never no more never no more.

Cigarette stink from a hole in the rushes
Dark as a dunny the under-runner
The green flax plaited for whiplashes
Cockabully finned with the fire of summer
Jack loves Jill on the garage door
Never no more never no more.

The trodden path in the brambles led
Sweet and sure to a lifted frock
To the boathouse spree and the hayloft bed
A hamstrung heart and no way back:
Like a toi-toi arrow shot in the air
Never no more never no more.

1952 *1952*

The Surfman's Story

On such a day as this
When breakers bay on the reef like a minutegun
    Or up the tall beach grind and hiss
    Like flattened snakes – we hauled out
    Tackle and lifeline, at the run,
For two swept seaward, bathers, caught in the current's rout.

    (There by the Maori Rock
A narrow rip runs out, rapid as death,
    Each tide, regular as the clock:
    Nothing to fear, once known – but a few
    Fool bathers drowned there a bad name bequeath
Till it grows to a gorgon myth, a cud for gossips to chew.)

    I stood by the reel
And Jake plunged in a smother of surf and sand.
    He could swim, that boy, like a river-eel;
    It was hard going even for his crawlstroke –
    I cursed the mad bathers, you'll understand.
Over his head the flurry of waves battered and broke.

    He told us after how
They beat him off; or rather the man did (she
    Was near sinking). He warded the blow,
    Trod water, waited; then by the hair
    Hauled her, a dead weight, from the treacherous sea
Back through the hurly-burly of breakers to earth and air.

    We worked for an hour to keep
The spark in her body alive; then gave her rum,
    Wrapt her in blankets to lie and sleep
    In the shed down there (the lupin and swordgrass
    Half hide it). But when she had come
To her senses it was only to yammer and cry *Alas*.

Like a dove that has lost its mate,
Or an eagle maybe (she had more that look
    In the full lip and nose knife-straight,
    Great cavernous eye) she'd have run back
    To the brawling sea if I hadn't took
Her by the arms and held her – the bruises stayed blue-black.

    It seemed they had made a pact
To drown together, impatient of Love's slow
    Guttering to death, and what life lacked
    For two fettered in wedlock, wild
    To wound each other – the undertow
Of passion drew them till it seemed the blind sea smiled.

    Well – he was washed ashore
Some weeks after, eaten by fishes, foul
    With tangleweed. She cried no more.
    We were married within the year: that house
    By the river's ours, with the climbing cowl
Of woodsmoke, the paddock behind, in a nest of orchard boughs.

1950–2 1952

Perseus

Leaving them, children of the Sun, to their perpetual
Unwearying dance about the ancient Tree,
Perseus flew east, the bird-winged sandals beating
Smooth and monotonous; sauntered above
Fens peopled by the placid watersnake,
Flamingo, crocodile –

And those unfallen creatures, joyful in
Their maze of waters, watched; with reedy voices
Praised the oncoming hero; cried
And coupled in his path. But he felt only
Scorching his shoulders, the shield, Athene's lovegift – and the first
Wind of foreboding blow from Medusa's home.

So entered the stone kingdom where no life
Startled, but brackish water fell
Like tears from solitary beds
Of sphagnum moss, or spray from cataracts
Sprinkled the grey-belled orchid, feathered grass
And spider's coverlet.

Till by the final cleft precipitous
At a blind gorge's end he lighted, stood,
Unslung the heavy shield, drew breath, and waited
As the bright hornet waits and quivers
Hearing within her den the poisonous rustle
And mew, for battle angry, of tarantula.

Fair smote her face upon the burning shield,
Medusa, image of the soul's despair,
Snake-garlanded, child of derisive Chaos
And hateful Night, whom no man may
Look on and live. In horror, pity, loathing,
Perseus looked long, lifted his sword, and struck.

Then empty was the cave. A vulture's taloned body
Headless and huddled, a woman's marble face
With snakes for hair – and in the wide
Thoroughfares of the sky no hint of cloudy fury
Or clanging dread, as homeward he
Trod, the pouched Despair at his girdle hanging,

To earth, Andromeda, the palace garden
His parents bickered in, plainsong of harvest –
To the lawgiver's boredom, rendering
(The task accomplished) back to benignant Hermes
And holy Athene goods not his own, the borrowed
Sandals of courage and the shield of art.

1952 1961

Spring Song

Tell Spring she is a whore
To flaunt her rags upon
Machinery of war
And the worse war within.
Death we had bargained for,
All monsters to be seen,
But not these tears of green.

The schoolboy twirls his cap;
Heifers low in the byre;
Stars in their orbits weep
And shake their manes of fire.
But O what urn of sleep
Offers us for love's food
These ashes blood-bedewed?

The migratory sun
Spins round the globe of dead:
All that our days have done,
All that our nights have fed,
Aches in the charred bone
Where in a funeral land
Our Hiroshimas stand.

Turn inward then your eyes.
From Naxos' angry beach
Forgetful Theseus rows,
Love's lucid power to teach
Left in the Bacchic maze;
Stony his breastplate gleaming,
At his prow the black sail booming.

The great ice-goddess of
An abstract myth
Contents our love
Where, numbed by her blizzard breath,
A climber's tactics have
Meaning; for there's no backward going
Alive to the grove of our spring denying.

1953, Hocken MS Book 17

Elegy at the Year's End

At the year's end I come to my father's house
Where passion fruit hang gold above an open doorway
And garden trees bend to the visiting bird:
      Here first the single vision
Entered my heart, as to a dusty room
Enters the pure tyrannical wind of heaven.

The coal burns out; the quiet ash remains
That tired minds and coarsened bodies know.
      Small town of corrugated iron roofs
Between the low volcanic saddle
And offshore reef where blue cod browse,
From husks of exile, humbled, I come to your fond prison.

At an elder uncle's deathbed I read the graph
Of suffering in the face of country cousins.
      These have endured what men hold in common,
The cross of custom, the marriage bed of knives;
Their angular faces reflecting his
Whose body lies stiff under the coverlet.

One may walk again to the fisherman's rock, hearing
The long waves tumble, from America riding
Where mottled kelpbeds heave to a pale sun,
      But not again see green Aphrodite
Rise to transfigure the noon. Rather the Sophoclean
Chorus: *All shall be taken.*

Or by the brown lagoon stand idle
Where to their haunted coves the safe flocks go,
And envy the paradise drake his brilliant sexual plumage.
      For single vision dies. Spirit and flesh are sundered
In the kingdom of no love. Our stunted passions bend
To serve again familiar social devils.

Brief is the visiting angel. In corridors of hunger
Our lives entwined suffer the common ill:
Living and dying, breathing and begetting.
Meanwhile on maimed gravestones under the towering fennel
Moves the bright lizard, sunloved, basking in
      The moment of animal joy.

1953 *1958*

Lament for Barney Flanagan

Licensee of the Hesperus Hotel

Flanagan got up on a Saturday morning,
Pulled on his pants while the coffee was warming;
He didn't remember the doctor's warning,
     'Your heart's too big, Mr Flanagan.'

Barney Flanagan, sprung like a frog
From a wet root in an Irish bog –
May his soul escape from the tooth of the dog!
     God have mercy on Flanagan.

Barney Flanagan R.I.P.
Rode to his grave on Hennessy's
Like a bottle-cork boat in the Irish Sea.
　　　　The bell-boy rings for Flanagan.

Barney Flanagan, ripe for a coffin,
Eighteen stone and brandy-rotten,
Patted the housemaid's velvet bottom –
　　　　'Oh, is it you, Mr Flanagan?'

The sky was bright as a new milk token.
Bill the Bookie and Shellshock Hogan
Waited outside for the pub to open –
　　　　'Good day, Mr Flanagan.'

At noon he was drinking in the lounge bar corner
With a sergeant of police and a racehorse owner
When the Angel of Death looked over his shoulder –
　　　　'Could you spare a moment, Flanagan?'

Oh the deck was cut; the bets were laid;
But the very last card that Barney played
Was the Deadman's Trump, the bullet of Spades –
　　　　'Would you like more air, Mr Flanagan?'

The priest came running but the priest came late
For Barney was banging at the Pearly Gate.
St Peter said, 'Quiet! You'll have to wait
　　　　For a hundred masses, Flanagan.'

The regular boys and the loud accountants
Left their nips and their seven-ounces
As chickens fly when the buzzard pounces –
　　　　'Have you heard about old Flanagan?'

Cold in the parlour Flanagan lay
Like a bride at the end of her marriage day.
The Waterside Workers' Band will play
　　　　A brass goodbye to Flanagan.

While publicans drink their profits still,
While lawyers flock to be in at the kill,
While Aussie barmen milk the till
      We will remember Flanagan.

For Barney had a send-off and no mistake.
He died like a man for his country's sake;
And the Governor-General came to his wake.
      Drink again to Flanagan!

Despise not, O Lord, the work of Thine own hands
And let light perpetual shine upon him.

1953 *1954*

To my Father

Dear friend, and more than dearest friend,
This day your message came to hand
And in return I rashly send
      This rhyming letter
Uncouthly made, goose-feather-penned
      In Burns's metre.

Above the hill, a curd in whey,
The moon rides in the nether sky,
Of Dionysiac poetry
      The Muse and mother;
She chills and kindles with her eye
      My heart's blown feather.

Often I've seen in the clouds' race
Her ancient, mottled, carline face
Bare to the winds of outer space,
      A deathshead staring
On human wit and human grace
      Cold and uncaring.

But now like Venus in her shell,
Not past the quarter, she bodes well
For man and beast, casting her spell
      O'er sea and land;
The winds that hurtled wild and snell
      Wait her command.

She folds the grey opossum brood
Within their havering holy wood
Where they may bicker, cough and feud
      Through night's green aisles;
The native owl his mate has woo'd
      Blessed by her smiles.

She peeks above the window glass
Where my two weans in slumber toss;
She glitters on the frosty grass
      Where unafraid
The hedgehogs on their errands pass
      From shade to shade.

The burglar's lantern she may be
Conniving at his felony,
Or light the buck who plants his knee
      On a maiden's sill,
Clear gazing through the hawthorn tree
      On good and ill.

She knows the tears in the secret bed
(Tears that immortals never shed)
For useless folly done or said
      And love outworn;
She strokes upon its dreamless head
      The child newborn.

At our two doors her fond light falls.
Yours are Laertes' garden-walls
Green and abiding, where fruit swells
        For earth's good reasons;
My own Ulysses' heart recalls
        With grief, gone seasons.

May our two minds the same light learn
With which Love's luminaries burn
And to the wrenching years return
        What time has taken –
As each for each rejoice and mourn
        With love unshaken.

                              1954, Hocken MS Book 18

The Giant's Grave

Some heavens ago, when the wind blew from a calmer
Airt, and stood yet Atlas, benignant Titan,
At the winged horizon's gate, his locks of cloud unshorn,
Heaving the sky on his shoulders – there deep in memory's glass,
Free of the torturer's hand, I and my elder brother
Walk the green riverbank in the land where I was born.

On one side, high ground ridged by cattletracks
Where our careering sledges would often whip from grassheads,
Before sunrise, a soaking dew; the beer-brown somnolent wave
Of the brackish river, cattleflats beyond it,
Brimmed sluggish under gorsepods; between them, a narrow tumulus,
Manuka-groved, broom-feathered, we called *The Giant's Grave*.

The horned beasts roared, ponderous at their crossing,
Dewlap-plunged in the dark stream; all night the reedy voices
Cried, *Aqua! Aqua!*, breaking the skin of sleep,
From ditch and bog; at noon the swampgrass flared
Smoke-pillared sacrifice, burned back to a stump of ashes
Beside Antaeus' bones in the grave-mound bedded deep.

In its rock flank a ngaio tree gave foothold,
Flesh-leaved, whose tarry buds breaking in flower sprinkled
Dust on an ageless mirror. There my brother laid
Lines for the basking eels, brutes thicker than a forearm,
Sailed his flaxstick navy, twig-masted on rough ripples
Flogged by desire's crosswind. Nothing made us afraid.

No, not fear of drowning, drawn down in weedy arms,
Nor any ghost dragging the eyes unwilling
To gaze on Adam's wound. Yet once, in a safe bed,
Sweating, chilled by nightmare, I saw a pyre kindled
On the river mound, and stark there, her face in anguish smiling,
Ablaze and unconsumed, my loved grandmother, dead.

1951–5 *1961*

Reflections on a Varsity Career

Friend or enemy, draw near;
Wellingtonians, lend an ear;
I too had a Varsity career
        In the early, early days.

I'll tell you nothing but the truth.
In the Queen City of the South
Our drinking habits were uncouth
        In the early, early days.

My thoughts were neo-pagan then.
I didn't belong to the s.c.m.
They didn't like me and I didn't like them
        In the early, early days.

I never held it was a sin
To sink a quart of orange gin.
On Thursday my weekend would begin
        In the early, early days.

Peculiar things were done and seen
In the Robert Burns and the Bowling Green.
God did not choose to intervene
          In the early, early days.

I liked to look at the birds and trees;
My textbooks gathered mould in peace;
I regarded swotting as a loathsome disease
          In the early, early days.

For recreation I played Slippery Sam
With a sailor on an oilboat from Abadan.
The johns caught up with him, poor man,
          In the early, early days.

My girlfriend had a flat of her own
With japanese tea-cups and fingerbones.
In a fortnight I lost half a stone
          In the early, early days.

Together we studied jet propulsion.
I never drank my Lane's Emulsion;
I avoided Psych. Prac. with revulsion
          In the early, early days.

Life went faster in '44.
I didn't have time to find it a bore
Between her place and the bottle store
          In the early, early days.

The lecturer's head was bald, of granite;
I admired the flies that skated upon it
And watched the clock shift minute by minute
          In the early, early days.

My cobber lived in Prince's Street.
The things we discussed I won't repeat.
There was lots to drink and little to eat
          In the early, early days.

Formal attire was seldom worn;
The parties kept on going till dawn
And saveloy skins were left on the lawn
        In the early, early days.

My relatives told me I'd wake with a bump
When I ended up on the rubbish dump;
But I lived like a camel off my hump
        In the early, early days.

Till the little green canary was eaten by the cat,
Till an octopus climbed from the brewer's vat,
Till the vulture squawked on the front door mat
        In the early, early days.

Ashes to ashes, dust to dust:
If the grog doesn't kill you, hard yacker must.
I think my physique was more robust
        In the early, early days.

Now my song must have an ending;
But you all must agree who have heard me sing
That a Varsity career is an excellent thing
        As it was for me in the early days,
        In the early, early days.

1956 *2001*

Crossing Cook Strait

The night was clear, sea calm; I came on deck
To stretch my legs, find perhaps
Gossip, a girl in green slacks at the rail
Or just the logline feathering a dumb wake.

The ship swung in the elbow of the Strait.
'Dolphins!' I cried – 'let the true sad Venus
Rise riding her shoals, teach me as once to wonder
And wander at ease, be glad and never regret.'

But night increased under the signal stars.
In the dark bows, facing the flat sea,
Stood one I had not expected, yet knew without surprise
As the Janus made formidable by loveless years.

His coat military; his gesture mild –
'Well met,' he said, 'on the terrestrial journey
From chaos into light – what light it is
Contains our peril and purpose, history has not revealed.'

'Sir – ', I began. He spoke with words of steel –
'I am Seddon and Savage, the socialist father.
You have known me only in my mask of Dionysus
Amputated in bar rooms, dismembered among wheels.

'I woke in my civil tomb hearing a shout
For bread and justice. It was not here.
That sound came thinly over the waves from China;
Stones piled on my grave had all but shut it out.

'I walked forth gladly to find the angry poor
Who are my nation; discovered instead
The glutton seagulls squabbling over crusts
And policies made and broken behind locked doors.

'I have watched the poets also at their trade.
I have seen them burning with a wormwood brilliance.
Love was the one thing lacking on their page,
The crushed herb of grief at another's pain.

'Your civil calm breeds inward poverty
That chafes for change. The ghost of Adam
Gibbering demoniac in drawing-rooms
Will drink down hemlock with his sugared tea.

'You feed your paupers concrete. They work well,
Ask for no second meal, vote, pay tribute
Of silence on Anzac Day in the pub urinal;
Expose death only by a mushroom smell.

'My counsel was naïve. Anger is bread
To the poor, their guns more accurate than justice,
Because their love has not decayed to a wintry fungus
And hope to the wish for power among the dead.

'In Kaitangata the miner's falling sweat
Wakes in the coal seam fossil flowers.
The clerk puts down his pen and takes his coat;
He will not be back today or the next day either.'

With an ambiguous salute he left me.
The ship moved into a stronger sea,
Bludgeoned alive by the rough mystery
Of love in the running straits of history.

1947–56 1958

Harry Fat and Uncle Sam

Said Uncle Sam to Harry Fat,
  'Your folks are fine to know
And it's great the way your island
  Keeps afloat there Down Below,
But you need the global attitude
  To produce a first-class show.'

'Just give me time,' said Harry Fat,
'And the tourist trade will grow.'

'It's not my place,' said Uncle Sam,
  'To give advice to you,
But you don't know how to break a strike
  Of monkeys in a zoo.
Our Company policemen could
  Teach yours a thing or two.'

'I'll change the Law,' said Harry Fat,
'It's an easy thing to do.'

'The dollar talks,' said Uncle Sam,
  'And you've a lot to learn.
How come you let your Varsity Reds
  Play possum in the fern
With no interrogations?
  Turn on the heat: they'll burn.'

'We'll start today,' said Harry Fat,
'And fry them each in turn.'

'Your folks don't know,' said Uncle Sam,
  'What entertainment means
For a trigger-happy tourist
  With a dollar in his jeans.
No whorehouse on the corner
  Was a grief to our Marines.'

'Try Mazengarb,' wrote Harry Fat,
'For some talent in the teens.'

'To tell you straight,' said Uncle Sam,
        'Your hotel service stinks.
Each dame should get an orchid
        At her table with the drinks;
And we're used to a Negro bellhop
        Who'll say sorry when he blinks.'

'Try Corbett next,' wrote Harry Fat,
'And find out what he thinks.'

'With a few things done,' said Uncle Sam,
        'I guess your country soon
Will make the grade – Jeepers! I'd like
        To hear a crooner croon
With an off-white broad beside me
        Under a Pig Island moon.'

'Bring dollars in,' said Harry Fat,
'And you can call the tune.'

1956 *1976*

A Rope for Harry Fat

Oh some have killed in angry love
  And some have killed in hate,
And some have killed in foreign lands
  To serve the business State.
The hangman's hands are abstract hands
  Though sudden death they bring –
'The hangman keeps our country pure,'
  Says Harry Fat the King.

Young love will kick the chairs about
  And like a rush fire burn,
Desiring what it cannot have,
  A true love in return.
Who knows what rage and darkness fall
  When lovers' thoughts grow cold?
'Whoever kills must pay the price,'
  Says Harry Fat the old.

With violent hands a young man tries
  To mend the shape of life.
This one used a shotgun
  And that one used a knife.
And who can see the issues plain
  That vex our groaning dust?
'The Law is greater than the man,'
  Says Harry Fat the just.

Te Whiu was too young to vote,
  The prison records show.
Some thought he was too young to hang;
  Legality said, *No.*
Who knows what fear the raupo hides
  Or where the wild duck flies?
'A trapdoor and a rope is best,'
  Says Harry Fat the wise.

Though many a time he rolled his coat
      And on the bare boards lay,
He lies in heavy concrete now
      Until the Reckoning Day.
In linen sheet or granite aisle
      Sleep Ministers of State.
'We cannot help the idle poor,'
      Says Harry Fat the great.

Mercy stirred like a summer wind
      The wigs and polished boots
And the long Jehovah faces
      Above their Sunday suits.
The jury was uncertain;
      The judge debated long.
'Let Justice take her rightful course,'
      Said Harry Fat the strong.

The butcher boy and baker boy
      Were whistling in the street
When the hangman bound Te Whiu's eyes
      And strapped his hands and feet,
Who stole to buy a bicycle
      And killed in panic blood.
'The parson won his soul at length,'
      Said Harry Fat the good.

Oh some will kill in rage and fear
      And some will kill in hate,
And some will kill in foreign lands
      To serve the master State.
Justice walks heavy in the land;
      She bears a rope and shroud.
'We will not change our policy,'
      Says Harry Fat the proud.

1956 *1961*

Husband to Wife

My sweet Medea, let us sing
    Below the dragon-guarded star:
We have two kids, hey-ding-a-ding,
    A flat, a fridge, a motor car.

Our regime, rational, humane,
    Ignores the savages' caprice;
But oh in dreams I sail again
    And labour for the Golden Fleece.

With an oar-roughened hand I grip
    Your playground of official sex;
Then to the chest-of-drawers I trip
    For diaphragm and Koromex.

And that good-humoured skirmish done,
    My space-men take their nuptial flight
Till their ships vanish one by one
    Devoured by contraceptive night.

Doomed from the start, so calm we'll land
    On Venus' tropic globe, and there
Found a new city out of hand,
    The death-ships rise, explode in air.

My fair Medea, do not doubt
    I love you with a love sincere;
More kids would strain our bank account
    And spoil your lovely figure, dear.

Yet I recall when out of sleep
    Your breasts flowed like the Milky Way.
I groaned, an axehead buried deep
    Below the turf of Breaker Bay.

The sense of quite unusual things
    Possessed my adolescent mind.
That mutual harmony Time brings
    I did not fully comprehend.

Our elder child is much too wild
    And he is why we married, dear.
Our younger one likes chewing gum
    And plaits and pulls her dolly's hair.

Yet even they grow day by day
    More contraceptively polite.
Sometimes I want to yell and grunt
    And like an apeman hug them tight.

But you, my mild Medea, with
    A lucid No would stop the dance.
You lead me from the sexual myth
    To a platonic tolerance.

1956, Hocken MS Book 18

In Fires of No Return

While bluegum fables burn
To summer's ash
In fires of no return
Above the farms and crying folds
That house the doom of flesh,
To Barney's pulpit rock I climb
Where the sea aisles burn cold
In fires of no return
And maned breakers praise
The death hour of the sun.
To wave and bird I open wide
The bible of my rimrock days,
To salt-grey ngaio boughs that cross

The forehead of the west,
To Venus' holy star who smiles
Upon the lives she cannot save,
Man, beast, bird, lover
In orchards of a spring desire,
Hermit old on his wintry pyre,
All flesh wound in the bright snare,
In fires of no return
Wrung by the power of the prince of the air.

My country fathers laid
Under angel and cold urn
In fields of silence burn,
From folds of ngaio and strong fern
Turn their immortal eyes on mine,
Tell me this day the world was made.
I hear in frond and shell
The voice of the drowned sailor
Tossed on the black bar, with a winy breath
Shout from the feast of Cana.
How love has raked the embers of his death.
And hermit from a holy cell
I watch my brother
King shag dive
Down from his windy
Rock to the humble tide
Where the sea poor, old crab and limpet,
Sigh to the resurrection thunder.
Among night dunes the moony lovers
In lupin shade far and near
Twined under Venus' carnal star
Mock the power of the prince of the air.
Their doomed flesh answers an undying summer.

1956 1958

By the Dry Cardrona

I can tell where cherries grow
    By the dry Cardrona,
Where I plucked them long ago
    On a day when I was sober.

My father wore a parson's coat
    By the dry Cardrona;
He kept a tally of the sheep and the goats,
    And I was never sober.

My mother sewed her Sunday skirt
    By the dry Cardrona,
They said she died of a broken heart
    For I was never sober.

O lay my bones till the judgement crack
    By the wild Cardrona!
The blanket swag upon my back
    Will pillow me drunk or sober.

I loved a girl and only one
    By the dry Cardrona:
She up and married the banker's son
    For I was never sober.

I courted a widow of forty-nine
    By the dry Cardrona,
She owned a stable and a scheelite mine
    But I was never sober.

All rivers run to the rimless grave,
    Even the wild Cardrona,
But the black cherry bent my way
    One day when I was sober.

1956 *1959*

At Hokianga

Green floating mangrove pods reveal,
Plucked from the lagging tide, their small
Man-in-a-boat, kernel and clitoris:
Set free to sail, they climb a hundred beaches,
Germinate in night-black mud. Tell,
Historian, how the broken tribes were healed
In a land of exhausted wells, north
From that great ragged capital
Flung like a coat to rot on garden earth.

In houses thatched with nikau palm,
Fearing the dead, riding bareback
On hill stallions, those who learned before us
The secret of survival, to be patient,
Suffer, and shut no doors,
Change all things to their habit, bridge
The bogs with branch laid to branch:
Nourished at compliant breasts, wish only
To drink with friends, own a launch.

To scrape the bones of the dead, how needful,
Lest they should walk, undo forgetfulness
With blight on crops, sickness at home.
In packed ground the missionary fathers
Drowned at river crossings, rest in one bed,
While a boy cuts from flax a spirit boat
Perfect, lightly as a bird's wing
Riding the void of waters
Untaught, a full hour floating.

1957 *1958*

Pyrrha

As kites rise up against the wind
Out of the past I summon Pyrrha,
Girl of plaited wheat, first
Mentor of love revealed in dying.

She has come back with a burning-glass
To whom once my thoughts clung
Like branches under weirs tumbling:
That freedom led to the lion's jaws,
A mind riddled by illusion.
The autumn sky is hers, a flooding
Trick of light on bars of broken cloud.

The streetlamp tells me where she lived.
Re-entering that square, untidy room
Where cups lie mixed with fingerbones
I find her again. Forehead too full,
Opaque blue eyes, bruised archaic smile
Dug from under shards. Pleasure,
A crab gripping the spine;
A mouth lent, not given;
Hair like marram grass, that made
On the short sofa, a burglar's tent.

Rib from my side, Pyrrha,
I who was young am older,
The wound healed, the flush of seed dry.
You cried once: 'I am drifting, drifting.'
Self-pitying, too often drunk,
I did not see your need of comforting.
Pestle and mortar pounded us
Early to a dry volcanic dust.

1957, Hocken MS Book 19

At Akitio

Consider this barbarian coast,
Traveller, you who have lost
Lover or friend. It has never made
Anything out of anything.
Drink at these bitter springs.

Fishing at river mouth, a woman
Uses the sea-drilled stone her mother used
For sinker, as big kahawai come,
As tides press upward to time's source.
This coast is shelter to the shearing gangs
Who burn dead matai in their kitchen.

Squirearch, straight-backed rider, built
An ethos of the leisured life,
Lawn, antlered hall and billiard room,
Glass candelabra brought from Paris,
The homestead foundered among fields.
Unhorsed they sleep.

A girl with a necklace of mako teeth
They dug from a sandcliff facing south,
Axe and broken needle.
Stay good under slab and cross
Thin bones of children burnt by cholera,
Made tidy by the last strict nurse.
As tributary of a greater stream
Your single grief enlarges now
The voice of night in kumara gardens,
Prayer of the bush pigeon.

One drowned at the cattle crossing,
One tossed and kicked by a bucking horse –
Who died without confession, wanting
No wafer in their teeth –
Does the toi-toi plume their altar?

Are they held safe in the sea's grail?
This gullied mounded earth, tonned
With silence, and the sun's gaze
On a choir of breakers, has outgrown
The pain of love. Drink,
Traveller, at these pure springs.

Remember, though, the early strength
Of bull-voiced water when the boom broke
And eels clung to the banks, logs
Plunged and pierced the river hymen.
Remember iron-coloured skulls
Of cattle thrown to the crab's crypt,
Driftwood piled by river flood
On the long beach, battered limb
And loin where the red-backed spider breeds,
By a halcyon sea the shapes of man,
Emblems of our short fever.

Pluck then from ledges of the sea
Crayfish for the sack. Not now but later
Think what you were born for. Drink,
Child, at the springs of sleep.

1957 *1958*

The Phoenix' Nest

Who can find the phoenix' nest
     Or the basilisk in his lair?
I have seen King Orion
     Fettered by a hair.

Let it hang below your shoulders,
     The gold Jason stole:
A jail to ease the body's pain,
     A cloister for my soul.

True or false, who'll wonder
     When we both are old?
One grief contains a thousand griefs,
     That joy runs cold.

Hearts turn to rock, my dear,
     Rock turns to sand.
The sandstone blows about the hills
     That were a pleasant land.

Do you but say, *I'd have it so*,
     And creeks will backward run,
Dead bones live, and this love last
     Beyond tomorrow's sun,

The stoniest mocker leave the street
     And climb our wooden stair,
To gaze on great Orion
     Tangled in your hair.

                    1957, Hocken MS Book 19

Song of the Years

When from my mother's womb I came
Disputandum was my name.

Weeping hoping threatening
Beyond myself I had no king.

I drew in with each hour's breath
The grey dust of the second death.

When my childhood days were spent
To Venus I grew suppliant.

Little tremors woke and died
Within the mountain of my pride.

Singing on the gallows cart
Created beauty held my heart.

The ardvaark and the onager
Were stabled at my sepulchre.

In that deep den the King of bliss
Broke my heart and gave me His.

'This for your doom and penance take,
Be merry always for My sake.'

He gave me a white stone to bear
With my true name written there.

Without end I will say,
Laus tibi, Domine!

1958 *1958*

Howrah Bridge

to my wife

Taller than the stair of Qtub Minar
These iron beams oppress the eagle's town.
Bare heels will dint them slowly.
And swollen Gunga's muscles move
Beneath, with freight of garbage,
Oar and sail, the loot of many lives.

In the unsleeping night my thoughts
Are millet falling from an iron pan,
While you, my dear, in Delhi lying down
Enter the same room by another door.
The rupee god has trampled here;
The poor implore a Marxist cage.
Dragon seed, the huddled bundles lying
In doorways have perhaps one chilli,
A handful of ground maize.
King Famine rules. Tout and owl-eyed whore
Whose talons pluck and stain the sleeve,
Angels of judgement, husk the soul
Till pity, pity only stays.

Out of my wounds they have made stars:
Each is an eye that looks on you.

1958 *1961*

School Days

I touch them with a word, so close they stand
After a thousand hours and days,
Older than Cocteau, in the dream museum
Of corridors and changing rooms:
A palace, jail and maze.

There I imbibed, as at a breast, truth
Beside the simple streams and elms;
England, my wet nurse, with her bitter milk.
So from sugared childhood came
On to the watershed of tears
With those small angular companions,
Handlers of the penis and the pen.

Hard to forgive them even now,
Precursors of the adult nightmare –
Franey, Nero of the dormitory,
Holmes, with the habits of a jaguar
And the sleek animal hide,
Waiting in a bend of the high stone stair.

Plunged early into the abyss of life
Where the tormentors move,
At war with God, the terrible Watcher,
An octopus behind a round glass window
With knives and justice, but no love.

That guilt grew wrongly, driven underground
With the first prickings of raw sense.
Yet there was friendship, comics, dominoes,
A dried newt like a bootsole in a drain,
New conkers like peeled testicles,
Sharing of exile, and the habit, pain.

The village like a mother stayed outside
With wells and horses, till the coat

Of manhood could be stitched and worn –
And the green mandrake Poetry
Born whole and shrieking one bleak night
Under stiff sheets and wincing at the dawn.

1958 *1974*

This Indian Morning

This Indian morning brown as Icarus
Flows guiltless to the vault of noon
Not influenced by cent per cent,
Obediences baggy at the seams,
Outside the Cretan labyrinth
Of money, conscience, work, glum dreams.

Now from the Muslim quarter rise
Dissolving cries and arabesques of fire
From braziers heated with dry cattle-dung.
Tomb-dwellers, women in black shawls,
With pots of dirty brass
Pad to the well, and chatter in the sun.

Eagles have bathed their wings at the ocean streams.
In a cold taxi coming from the mass
With Bertha in her blue silk dress
I think of money. Lepers in the gateway
Hold out their cups and bandaged palms.
Their eyes like desert cisterns burn.
Each soul a moonless oubliette
Waiting for the last great Key to turn.

1959 *1961*

Night in Delhi

The moon's vast geometric nimbus
Includes the town, the tombs, the heavy eaves
As cold as Rome and twice as foreign.
At night the cages of the past open,
Love shakes the safe dwelling.
Bar the thin door to keep out thieves.

I want simplicity and lightness
To break these daily fetters and
Thoughts that move like Delhi oxen
Gaunt-ribbed, with gold-painted horns,
Hauling the load of endless noon.
The empire of a poem gladly
Would hide beneath your hand.

We broach the midnight of the Kama Sutra
(Mare's hold, spear-thrust, split-bamboo,
Crab and blossoming lotus)
Nudging from the earth of many wishes
While under flowered quilts the children sleep.
Unbind your dark hair. Seas of the heart
Drawn by the nearness of the moon
Into prodigious waterspouts. These
Were our familiar proud catastrophes
That spilt upon the rock a rain of fishes.

I saw where in a wilderness did lie
The royal spirits of our burdened age.
Some slept; some roared, and shook the walls in rage;
Crowned beasts in cages open to the sky.
The lucky ones are mated. O my queen,
Here is your mortal canopy and throne.
We are two eagles in an equal gyre
Rising above the wilds of sense
In the sun's eye and freedom of his grove.
Such love seems to the world indifference.

1959 *1961*

Be Happy in Bed

One landscape, many women:
Ambition of that savage empty boy
Haunting the bathing sheds and diamond bay,
Composing verses in an upstairs room.
Now the long windings of a broken sense
In humorous elegiacs write his doom.

Boathouses on the edge of Nowhere
Recur to trouble after-dinner sleep,
White legs among the cords and rowlocks –
'There is a spirit in the moving water
Forgives and understands us
Though God has gone inside and slammed the door.'
Where the boats ride endlessly
Grip and hold the sea king's daughter.

Sex taught him sadness: like St Lawrence
Roasting on the grid of conscience:
'One side is brown; now try the other.'
The self so persecuted by enigmas
Prefers a mountain to a nagging mother.

Put off the past: you have endured it,
Enjoyed, or else confessed it.
This luxury like cut veins in a bath
Stains too much the moving water.
No meaning now in that direction
Though skeletons toward the salt pans creep.
The age of sex, the age of centaurs
Returns to punish after-dinner sleep.

1958–9 *1979*

Elephanta

Accordion and sweet brisk drum
Waken a lounging passion

Outside the wooden teashop where a young
Black-trousered androgynous dancer

Trounces the dust, crooking a maggot's finger,
While pockmarked queers applaud and smoke.

Great hawks like monoplanes
Above the bony tamarind,

Above the quarried rock sail high, high,
And Shiva like a business uncle watches

The village girls with cans to fill
File through the temple to a covered cistern.

Consider. Seasnake, white cloud minnow,
Octopus and moray eel,

Lovely in their lit aquariums
Breathe water as we do,

Have the advantage that they cannot feel.
Yet I have seen, across an angry tide-rip,

The narrow coffin-boat, the catamaran,
Go simply as a girl, with forward-leaning

Mast and torn triangular sail,
Leaving a crowded net behind.

1959 *1961*

Return to Exile

Returning on shipboard from an older land,
Amoeba in his bowels, one travelling man
Sees with gratitude the home coast rise,
Lares et penates ...

No trumpet on the mountain. From
Exile into exile he goes home.
Secretly the glittering coast instructs him:
'Your lot is now intelligible pain.
Ignore the whorish voice that whispers
Of meekness, meekness among thieves.
I am your angel. Rage against me.
Older, so very little wiser,
Set down your meaning with a shaking hand.'

                    1959–60, Hocken MS Book 20

Mr Baxter's Evening Liturgy

Coals crack. Frost glazes the back step.
Long rains and heavy push down stones
To the scouring creek. Ah well,
It's good to be back
From India. My wife in slacks
And tree-brown jersey bends her bones
Incredibly to read – NO ONE IN HELL,
PARSON'S STATEMENT: BISHOP DISAGREES.
The coal fumes make me sneeze.
Beggars, tombs and banyan trees
Stand up in Delhi. Soon we'll both retire
From the red, clinkered fire
And dream of porcupines. Till day.
Timor mortis non conturbat me.

                    1959 *1976*

Spring Song of a Civil Servant

In corridor and cubicle
The vine is pulling bricks apart
Underneath my fishbone armour
Beats a wild Othello's heart
And between the cup and saucer

Many a savage dream is born
Of Desdemona's eyeballs popping
Fantasy ah fantasy
Above my dome the flies hedge hopping
Come to a perfect three point landing

Nevertheless notwithstanding
Eighteen hundred memoranda
A girl with sand inside her socks
Would find me ready to philander
But my Sunday spouse awaits

Car key door key vacuum cleaner
And the Lions cannot win
Caged up in Athletic Park
Tonight I'll have a double gin
The outlook for the id is dark.

1959 *1976*

THE 1960s

Otago Daily Times

The success of *The Wide Open Cage* in the late 1950s inspired Baxter to write two further plays: *Three Women and the Sea* (1961) and *The Spots of the Leopard* (1962). His first major poetry publication of the 1960s was a broadsheet that would come to be one of his most enduring social critiques, *Ballad of Calvary Street*. This was followed in 1961 by *Howrah Bridge and Other Poems*, a collection that is an icon of the tremendous changes, personal and poetic, he went through in the late 1950s – changes brought into focus by the months he spent in Asia in 1958–9. The poems in India mark this change. Stylistically, the Indian poems reflect the strong influence of Lawrence Durrell.

In 1963 Baxter became a postman. He produced a number of polemical poems, many protesting against the Vietnam War. Themes inherited from his pacifist parents, and explored in his unpublished adolescent verse, were reworked to satiric effect in such poems as 'A Bucket of Blood for a Dollar' and 'The Gunner's Lament'. *Poetry Magazine* in Wellington published *A Selection of Poetry* in 1964, but Baxter's next major collection was the widely praised *Pig Island Letters* (1966).

Pig Island Letters' title sequence, dedicated to his friend, the author Maurice Shadbolt, identifies with Shadbolt's despondency at an apparent loss of creativity, before taking gloomy inventory of his own failed undertakings. Typically, lost youth is mourned and death looms large in the future, yet the poems also achieve a new, less censorious, realism – of which 'Pig Island', Baxter's colloquial, amiably caustic name for New Zealand, is emblematic. The collection fully anticipates the Jerusalem poetry as Baxter further develops his notion of the 'gap' – that paradoxical site of absence within which one discovers the true self – and prefigures a full adoption of the role of social prophet by diagnosing society's maladies through a rehearsal of the dramas of his own life. The critic C.K. Stead, who savagely criticised *In Fires of No Return*, was won over by this volume, describing its 'total effect [as] richer than anything Baxter had achieved before'.

From 1966 to 1967 Baxter was Burns Fellow in creative writing at the University of Otago. It was a triumphant homecoming for the man who had left twenty years earlier under a cloud of failure. Baxter took an active part in university life, protesting against Vietnam and satirising the university prohibition against student cohabitation in his pamphlet *A Small Ode on Mixed Flatting*. Through all this his creative output was staggering: he wrote numerous poems, and published a selection, *The Lion Skin: Poems* (1967), through the university's Bibliography Room.

Revisiting the site of his painful but formative adolescence also impelled Baxter to revisit, in his poetry, the themes and locales of the verse of that period. Family memories and Otago landscapes again feature, but always with the presence of death, at times subtly, at other times looming, within the poetic frame. A marked change in style accompanied these variations on familiar themes, as if the earlier artifice and abstraction has been deliberately stripped out so that all that remains is a personal voice described by the poet and critic Vincent O'Sullivan as 'almost ostentatiously matter of fact'.

In 1967, Baxter also published two volumes of criticism – *Aspects of Poetry in New Zealand* and *The Man on the Horse* – and saw a number of his plays and mimes staged by Dunedin director Patric Carey, among them *The Band Rotunda*, *The Sore-Footed Man*, *The Bureaucrat* and *The Devil and Mr Mulcahy*. Just as Baxter's verse supplied several of the characters for these dramas, so his experiences as an alcoholic and working with alcoholics supplied a usefully emblematic 'tribal' context within which human frailties were examined through a mythical, or archetypal, lens. Most of Baxter's drama is in Howard McNaughton's edition of his *Collected Plays* (1982).

In 1968 Dunedin's Catholic Education Office employed Baxter to prepare catechetical material and teach at Catholic schools, and his articles for the Catholic periodical *The Tablet* were collected and published in *The Flowering Cross* (1969). Yet the Burns Fellowship appeared to have drained him of energy and refilled him with doubt. He struggled in his marriage, fearing the trap of domesticity; found difficulty relating to his children; and was dogged by the feeling that words had become impotent and should be replaced by actions.

Around April 1968 'a minor revelation' led him to think of Jerusalem (in Māori 'Hiruharama') – 'the mission station on the Wanganui River'. He thought he might go to this small Māori settlement, bordered by a Catholic church and a convent, and 'form the nucleus of a community where the people, both Maori and pakeha [*sic*], would try to live without money or books, worship God and work on the land'. Following the family's return to Wellington in December, Baxter left home to put his beliefs into practice.

Auckland was his initial stop. He failed to hold down a job which the poet Hone Tuwhare had found for him there, at the Chelsea sugar refinery. He discovered his Auckland niche in a cluster of run-down squats in the suburb of Grafton. Number 7, Boyle Crescent, where he settled in Easter 1969, became a drop-in centre for drug addicts. Baxter, adopting the Māori transliteration of his first name, 'Hemi', set about counselling and attempting to establish a Narcotics Anonymous organisation similar to AA. His appearance – barefoot, bearded and shabbily dressed – attracted the attention of both media and police, who suspected his motives and morality. He put the drug users' side of the story in 'Ballad of the Junkies and the Fuzz', and also published a selection of twenty years' verse in *The Rock Woman* (1969).

The Rock Woman's fifty-three poems were largely chosen by Baxter's English publisher, Oxford University Press. Baxter approved the choices, which were intended to provide an overview of his achievements during the preceding two decades, but critics have commented on a certain unevenness in the book. The title poem refers to a rock, found on the coast, that resembles a woman. The drops of seawater that cover her are reminiscent of the rosary beads found on a medieval statue. For Baxter, the Rock Woman also symbolised New Zealand's bare, stony landscapes, which were for him as familiar as a lover – alone with her, he experienced peace.

But poetry was not Baxter's main focus at this time. By August 1969, the Boyle Crescent period had ended and he was heading for Jerusalem, to form his commune.

The Sixties

for Louis Johnson

'The icy dawn of the sixties' —
Yes, you have it there.
Today I saw a black sperm whale
Rolled on the rocks at Pukerua Bay.

The stench grew loud as I came near,
Gulls were grabbing at the kill.
From that sleek projectile body
Jutted a gigantic reddened phallus
Mauled by the Cook Strait squid.

Under the sunset fires it seemed to be
The body of our common love
That bedrooms, bar rooms never killed,
The natural power behind our acts and verses
Murdered by triviality.

1960 *1961*

Ballad of Calvary Street

On Calvary Street are trellises
Where bright as blood the roses bloom,
And gnomes like pagan fetishes
Hang their hats on an empty tomb
Where two old souls go slowly mad,
National Mum and Labour Dad.

Each Saturday when full of smiles
The children come to pay their due,
Mum takes down the family files
And cover to cover she thumbs them through,
Poor Len before he went away
And Mabel on her wedding day.

The meal-brown scones display her knack,
Her polished oven spits with rage,
While in Grunt Grotto at the back
Dad sits and reads the Sporting Page,
Then ambles out in boots of lead
To weed around the parsnip bed.

A giant parsnip sparks his eye,
Majestic as the Tree of Life;
He washes it and rubs it dry
And takes it in to his old wife –
'Look Laura, would that be a fit?
The bastard has a flange on it!'

When both were young she would have laughed,
A goddess in her tartan skirt,
But wisdom, age and mothercraft
Have rubbed it home that men like dirt:
Five children and a fallen womb,
A golden crown beyond the tomb.

Nearer the bone, sin is sin,
And women bear the cross of woe,
And that affair with Mrs Flynn
(It happened thirty years ago)
Though never mentioned, means that he
Will get no sugar in his tea.

The afternoon goes by, goes by,
The angels harp above a cloud;
A son-in-law with spotted tie
And daughter Alice fat and loud
Discuss the virtues of insurance
And stuff their tripes with trained endurance.

Flood-waters hurl upon the dyke
And Dad himself can go to town,
For little Charlie on his trike
Has ploughed another iris down.
His parents rise to chain the beast,
Brush off the last crumbs of their lovefeast.

And so these two old fools are left,
A rosy pair in evening light,
To question Heaven's dubious gift,
To hag and grumble, growl and fight:
The love they kill won't let them rest,
Two birds that peck in one fouled nest.

Why hammer nails? Why give no change?
Habit, habit clogs them dumb.
The Sacred Heart above the range
Will bleed and burn till Kingdom Come,
But Yin and Yang won't ever meet
In Calvary Street, in Calvary Street.

1960 *1960*

Evidence at the Witch Trials

No woman's pleasure did I feel
    Under the hazel tree
When heavy as a sack of meal
    The Black Man mounted me,
But cold as water from a dyke
    His seed that quickened me.

What his age I cannot tell;
    Foul he was, and fair.
There blew between us both from Hell
    A blast of grit and fire,
And like a boulder is the babe
    That in my womb I bear.

Though I was youngest in that band
    Yet I was quick to learn.
A red dress he promised me
    And red the torches burn.
Between the faggot and the flame
    I see his face return.

1956–60 1961

Christchurch 1948

The true town will evade your map,
Murderous, choked by its cathedral stone.
Those granite jowls I remember,
A.'s hornet nest of Yeatsian prose,
D. flattened in a chair, dead drunk on gin,
A vague fog rising from the Avon,
A city founded in wanhope
And English, English, English to the bone.

Hunger for light sustained me there
Under the sign of Dionysus-Hades,
In a kennel with a torn gas mantle,
Alive on milk and benzedrine,
Haruspex, probing the flight of birds.
Once came an old man with a rotting face,
And more than once my girl, to squeeze
Kisses out, cool whey from curds.

The founding father in his stovepipe hat
Watched, but could not understand
My rage, her sweet potato beauty.
The bells implored us to die soon.
Sickles of foam on winter beaches
In their angelic speech instructed
Two children sighing in the labyrinth
For light, for the country of high noon.

1960 *1961*

Winter

Winter unbundles a sack of storms
Above the flat scrub country.

Far at sea a trawling captain
Watches a double rainbow arching,
Noah's good sign, along the black horizon,
Hopes for groper, fat cod, terakihi.

A bureaucrat lights the gas fire
That warms his raw-edged afternoon,
Plucks a folder from a grey steel file,
Coughs, and eyes the telephone.

A housewife sees her washing, three-days-wet,
Hang draggled in the tugging wind,
Measures the old chair for new covers,
An ache of winter in the mind.

A child dawdling home from school
Builds little twig dams in the gutter,
Sings to himself although his shoes
Are damp, and bullies lurk at Butcher's Corner.

Winter unwraps a parcel of stones
For old and sick and sad, and homeless walkers.

1960 *1974*

To Our Lady of Perpetual Help

Mother, below my life you live,
Nurse of the unlucky ones:
Some old square-headed cabbage-eating priest
Bedragoned by arthritis, or a girl
Who has not found a single trusty man,
All who howl in the rusty frying pan.

Mother, I have no hope unless
You bring me in your holy apron
Clean to the garden gate. Mary, raise
Us who walk the burning slum of days
Not knowing left from right. I praise
Your bar room cross, your star of patience.

1960 *1961*

On the Death of her Body

It is a thought breaking the granite heart
Time has given me, that my one treasure,
Your limbs, those passion-vines, that bamboo body

Should age and slacken, rot
Some day in a ghastly clay-stopped hole.
They led me to the mountains beyond pleasure

Where each is not gross body or blank soul
But a strong harp the wind of genesis
Makes music in, such resonant music

That I was Adam, loosened by your kiss
From time's hard bond, and you,
My love, in the world's first summer stood

Plucking the flowers of the abyss.

1960 *1961*

Election 1960

Hot sun. Lizards frolic
Fly-catching on the black ash

That was green rubbish. Tiny dragons,
They dodge among the burnt broom stems

As if the earth belonged to them
Without condition. In the polling booths

A democratic people have elected
King Log, King Stork, King Log, King Stork again.

Because I like a wide and silent pond
I voted Log. That party was defeated.

Now frogs will dive and scuttle to avoid
That poking idiot bill, the iron gullet:

Delinquent frogs! Stork is an active King,
A bird of principle, benevolent,

And Log is Log, an old time-serving post
Hacked from a totara when the land was young.

1960 *1961*

A Dentist's Window

I, a boat with a bony keel,
Founder in waters of the afternoon,

Tilted back on the frightful chair
While Dr Gorodowski chooses

The perfect hornet drill.
High up on a pigeon-turded shelf

Above St Mary's canyon wall
Our Lady's concrete statue smiles

On floosies, taxi-drivers, psychopaths,
The whole rough stumble-footed town.

Lady, Lady, I am growing old,
My feathers moult, my prayers are cold,

Remember me today and when I die.
Take Dr Gorodowski by the hand,

Keep the drill's edge off the little nerve.
More than the rot of venial sin

I fear the stab, the graunch, the touch of metal.

1960 *1961*

To a Samoan Friend

Albert Wendt

As those cold waters rise at Rainbow Springs
Endlessly from the underworld
(So deep a fountain that the divers cannot
Find its beginning in the groins of earth;
So strong a current that the coins they drop
Spin sideways onto ledges) –

As those fish-breeding waters flow
Under tidy bridges,
Over white choking roots, through ditches
Where willows trail their leaves in shallows
For fretful girls on holiday –

So the creative current of your mind
Rises and flows in this dry land
Bringing to one or two the taste of peace.

1961 *1964*

At Raspberry Hut

Ice cold and clear
The water from the mitred mountain.
The black mare of rock
Neighs to the sky stallion.

1961 *1964*

The Rubber Monkey

Very late at night my son's red monkey
Crouches on the bookshelf, ready
To beat a tom-tom automatically

If you squeeze the bulb. It is
A relevant emblem. Operation Phoebus
Equally rubs out stupidities

And honourable speeches. There will come
From radio dials a speechless hum,
The rubber monkey whacks his drum

And mushrooms grow above the cities
Cruelly dissolving in their furnace
The powers of youth and age, the flask of pities.

1961 *1964*

A Family Photograph 1939

Waves bluster up the bay and through the throat
Of the one-span bridge. My brother shoots
The gap alone
Like Charon sculling in his boat
Above the squids and flounders. With the jawbone
Of a sperm whale he fights the town,
Dances on Fridays to the cello
With black-haired sluts. My father in his gumboots
Is up a ladder plucking down
The mottled autumn-yellow
Dangling torpedo clusters
Of passion fruit for home-made wine.
My mother in the kitchen sunshine
Tightens her dressing gown,
Chops up carrots, onions, leeks,
For thick hot winter soup. No broom or duster
Will shift the English papers piled on chairs
And left for weeks.
I, in my fuggy room at the top of the stairs,
A thirteen-year-old schizophrene,
Write poems, wish to die,
And watch the long neat mason-fly
Malignantly serene
Arrive with spiders dopier than my mind
And build his clay dungeons inside the roller blind.

1961 *1967*

The Tree

Nothing was evil then. The editing came later.
Thirty years back, down time's rock shaft, I see,
Too early for the heart-and-arrow sign,
A tree of vulvas oozing golden resin
Where I and my wire-muscled cousin
Climbed endlessly. Its bird-shit-spattered branches
Invoked the gross maternal mystery
That fed his life and mine.

Smoking my father's tobacco in a sly
Tree house, or edging up a shaking mast
To a cradle open to the sky,
Riding those giant fronded arms,
I seemed to be included by
The wind in its long conversation
About some secret known to birds or men;
Perhaps what made my uncle die;

Something too hard for words. My cousin,
Climbing the ladder after me,
Would call me barmy, slither down the tree
Like an opossum, wrestle with
Scissors and headlock, order me to try on
His boxing gloves. And fighting him
I quite forgot I carried in my pocket
Green macrocarpa nuts, the seeds of time.

1962 *1976*

The Bureaucrats

Like salamanders we don't realize
The element we live in — Us

Bureaucrats I mean. A tight
Cramp like the impulse to masturbate

Squeezes me as I tilt back on the chair
Of bent tubes and sponge rubber

Between the loaded desk and the door shut
By a forgotten choice. It is not

New: this nausea, a flicker of
Cold fire. My wife's photograph

With canoes in her eyes, and a steel crucifix
Pinned on the wall, shatter the reflex

That yielded for an instant to the invisible flame
Of nothingness. Caesar is not. I am.

1962 *1976*

At Serrières

Blue water of the Rhône in its rock bed
Stalling, circling in pools behind
The island lousy with snakes: down I sank
With stones inside my bathing dress
To the mud bottom, to walk like a crab,

All that green summer drank
Air, knowledge. Bitter tough-skinned grapes
In a wild hilltop vineyard,
And the days, the days, like long loaves
Broken in half, as I fished with a cord

And a pierced stone for Yvette, the manager's daughter,
Killing hens in the hotel courtyard.
That castle where my brother broke his arm,
Yes: convolvulus vines, starved ghosts in dungeons ...
But the family album does not include

The new guitar of sex I kept on twanging
Inside the iron virgin
Of the little smelly dyke, or that Easter Sunday,
Through a chink in the bedclothes, watching my mother dressing:
The heavy thighs, the black bush of hair.

Those wild red grapes were bitter
Though you could not tell them, by just looking, from the table
                                                                    kind.

                                                        1962 *1974*

The Hollow Place

On the waste low headland
Below the road, above the plunging sea,
I would climb often round the crumbling face
Where flax bushes precariously
Gave something to grip: then I'd stand
Alive in the hollow place
That meant ... well, I must describe it: a bent cleft
In limestone rock above a pool
Of fluttering scum; bushes to the left,
And an overhang. The passage was dark and cool,
Three yards long perhaps, hidden from any eye
Not acquainted; and the air
Tainted by some odour as if the earth sweated
In primeval sleep. I did nothing there;
There was nothing to do but listen to some greater I
Whose language was silence. Again and again I came
And was healed of the daftness, the demon in the head

And the black knot in the thighs, by a silence that
Accepted all. Not knowing I would come again,
My coat of words worn very thin,
Knocking, as if lame,
With a dry stick on the dumb
Door of the ground, and crying out:
'Open, mother. Open. Let me in.'

1962 *1966*

The Dying Nazi Guard

Mother, your hands are red,
Speckled like salami ... The little black hen died;
We fed her gobbets of bread
In the carved coop where you painted
Gottes gute gabe, under the sycamore
Whose whirling seeds are planes shot
Down in the Fuhrer's War ... The Fuhrer lied
When he promised us the Rhinegold, hot,
Burning our fingers. At Buchenwald
I hoisted the young Jew
Up by the thumbs till the swine sweated blue
With a pine cone in his arse ... The door
Won't shut against the unburied ones who stink
All day. At Buchenwald
The Christ-Child walks the barracks, blue and thin,
With bread for someone else's sin,
And I am Buchenwald. These foul sheets smother;
They are hoisting me up, Mother!
Your schnapps is Jewish blood; I cannot drink.

1962 *2001*

The Town under the Sea

The town was usual enough: it had
A creek, a bridge, a beach, a sky
Over it, and even a small tin church
I never went to. My brother, my cousins and I
Did what boys do – dozed in the hot

Schoolroom, made bows and arrows, dodged the mad
Boatbuilder, crept like rabbits through the black
Under-runner with a weak torch,
Burnt dry rushes, wrestled or swam,
Doing nothing important. The difference, looking back,

Was that we did not see our own
Death in an oil-fouled seagull's death,
And the copulation of dogs did not
Remind us of ourselves. At puberty,
Or the first deadly sin, the sea rose up in one

Pounding night and swallowed the land. Shark
And octopus triumph in the dark
Doors of the human breath,
And the spider-crab is strong. Kelp-bladders, tangled, thrown
Up by the cannibal sea

Glitter immense. My father's gun,
My mother's gold ring,
And that toy lamb I lost and wept for, lie inaccessible, deep
Among the bivalves. Nor do any
Bells ring, on a windy day, from those wide

Guts of the coffin-making tide.
It is a natural sleep.
Yet some have said (not fools, not ruled by money)
Beyond this dying world and the prison house
Of Purgatory, a land lies

Lovely for human eyes, where smashed love, broken vows,
Are healed again. Water must
Exist (they say) to answer thirst;
Our thirst is great. That second Paradise
We measure by the first.

1962 1979

Home Thoughts

I hate this boneyard peace
Of ceremonious dying, where
My mother, squat, strong-minded, with white hair,
Watches thc iceland poppies catch the breeze
Delicately. I hate and love
The tree of time, the dusty wattle grove,
And the blind devil on the stair
Who guarded and still guards the spidered room
That I wrote poems in. It seemed more safe to drown
ln the fat pubs of the harbour town
And rummage in the ash-pit
Of God, for some live coal to light the gloom;

Indeed no child of Adam wished
Only for peace. The thought of it
Is death. I see the rainbow stand above
Those troubled waters where I fished too long,
Too late, and caught
Leviathan. I hate and love
That garden where my father taught
Me early, yes, too early how
The cut worm must forgive the spade, the plough,
Or grafted apple twigs on stumps of hawthorn.
Wrong, right; right, wrong;
In contradiction, lady, I was born.

1962 1976

The Cold Hub

Lying awake on a bench in the town belt,
Alone, eighteen, more or less alive,
Lying awake to the sound of clocks,
The railway clock, the Town Hall clock,
And the Varsity clock, genteel, exact
As a Presbyterian conscience,
I heard the hedgehogs chugging round my bench,
Colder than an ice-axe, colder than a bone,
Sweating the booze out, a spiritual Houdini
Inside the padlocked box of winter, time and craving.

Sometimes I rolled my coat and put it under my head,
And when my back got frozen, I put it on again.
I thought of my father and mother snoring at home
While the fire burnt out in feathery embers.
I thought of my friends each in their own house
Lying under blankets, tidy as dogs or mice.
I thought of my med. student girlfriend
Dreaming of horses, cantering brown-eyed horses,
In her unreachable bed, wrapped in a yellow quilt,

And something bust inside me, like a winter clod
Cracked open by the frost. A sense of being at
The absolute unmoving hub
From which, to which, the intricate roads went.
Like Hemingway, I call it *nada*:
Nada, the Spanish word for nothing.
Nada; the belly of the whale; *nada*;
Nada; the little hub of the great wheel;
Nada; the house on Cold Mountain
Where the east and the west wall bang together;
Nada; the drink inside the empty bottle.
You can't get there unless you are there.
The hole in my pants where the money falls out,
That's the beginning of knowledge; *nada*.

It didn't last for long; it never left me.
I knew that I was *nada*. Almost happy,
Stiff as a giraffe, I called in later
At an early grill, had coffee, chatted with the boss.

That night, drunk again, I slept much better
At the bus station, in a broom cupboard.

1961–2 *1966*

Martyrdom

Balancing on two boards up under
The spouting I fiddle with a brush.
My wife tells me I'm slow;
I just wonder
Will Our Lady grab me if I dive
Thirty feet
Down like a bull seal to the concrete?
I doubt it.
In the kitchen she sings, 'Ko tenei te po,'
Like an Opunake thrush.
My rigours make her thrive;
I'm gaining merit.
My daughter grizzles down below
About some bad word someone said, or that
Fat plaster-eating mouse
Who camps under my bed.
She thinks I'm an acrobat
In a travelling show. This night. My son
Brings me a spider in a bottle – red
Like old burnt clay its hypodermic head –
Look, Daddy, look! The house
Of Atreus glitters in the midday sun.

1961–2 *1979*

The Iron Cradle

from Baudelaire

Get well fonged. The whole world's there outside your skin;
it's the one thing that matters. In order not to feel the terrible
swag of time cracking your shoulder-blades, and pushing
you down to the earth like a loaded branch – get well fonged.
Don't give yourself a break.
Don't worry about the label on the bottle. There's grog, poetry,
even virtue. Take your pick; as long as you get fonged on it.
And if for a minute, or a minute-and-a-half, on the steps of
the Post Office, or in the long grass beside the cable car,
or worst of all, in your own flat, you start to wake up
and the fong begins to shift – Ask the wind, the waves of
the harbour, birds, clocks, the stars in the sky, whatever
rolls, speaks, cries out, murmurs, runs away; ask
them what time it is, and they'll all answer –
'Time to get well fonged! There's no other way out of the
iron cradle. Grog or poetry, or even virtue – whatever
you like, go and get well fonged on it.'

1962 *2001*

Father to Son

Childish in me to appreciate
So much your approval, when you let
Me squeeze into your 'fort'

In the abandoned railway house
With smashed windows where you
Uncovered the necessary secret space
Just by lifting a board –

I should not care. Better for you
If I take no shelter with you
(There is not room for two

In one life) and I, being elder,
Must be myself a bomb shelter
To wife, child, friend, not digging for
Payment of approval. No.

How terrible if you should see my need
In the space inside where the dying 'I' bleeds,
And be disconcerted,

Saying, 'Aren't you happy?' Not long
After you were born (O star of beginning
In the black sliding pit) I would swing
Clumsily out of bed

To give you your bottle. Half-boozed
I had the sweet joy of being used
By one who did not ask

Where I had been, whether my hands were clean,
But was glad to be held and fed.
Such joy must be dissembled, my dear son,
By holding its light in a husk

Of indifference, a dark lantern,
Lest it should too brightly burn.
To be a father

Needs most of all, I think, an easy touch:
Better by far to clown too much,
Loudly break wind, visit your fort when requested,
Than to usurp the sighs of a mother.

1962 *2001*

To Any Young Man who Hears my Verses Read
in a Lecture Room

When some cheese-headed ladder-climber reads
     A poem of mine from the rostrum,
Don't listen. That girl in her jersey and beads,
     Second row from the front, has the original nostrum

I blundered through nine hundred parties and ninety-eight pubs
     In search of. The words are a totem
Erected long after for scholars and yobs
     Who'd make, if they could, a bicycle-seat of my scrotum.

          1963 *1979*

An Ode to the Reigning Monarch on the Occasion of
Her Majesty's Visit to Pig Island

Madam, I beg to quarrel with
Your trip across the water –
Pig Island needs no English myth
To keep its guts in order,
Though our half-witted housewives yearn
At your image on the TV screen.

Forgive me that I cannot praise
The Civil Service State
Whose blueprints falsify the maze
It labours to create,
And plants above that sticky mess
Yourself in an icing sugar dress.

The dead who drink at Bellamys
Are glad when school kids clap
A Fairy Queen who justifies
The nabob and the bureaucrat,
In a land where a wharfie's daughter can
Marry some day the squatter's son.

While the stuffed monkey, dog and sow,
Play ludo in the void,
The Auckland pavements carry now
Six hundred unemployed,
And the bought clerks who sneer at them
Will crowd to kiss your diadem.

The girls in Arohata jail
Are very rarely dressed in silk –
Let us take a Glasgow cocktail
Bubbling coal gas into milk,
Drink up to Mary, Kate and Lou,
No better and no worse than you.

Before my birth your soldiers made
A football of my skull
At Mud Farm when they crucified
My father on a pole
Because he would not take a gun
And kill another working man.

I give you now to end our talk
A toast you will not like:
MacSweeney the Lord Mayor of Cork
Who died on hunger strike.
It took him eighty days to drown
In the blood and shit that floats the Crown.

While Big Ben bangs out stroke on stroke
And the circus wheel spins round,
The Maori looks at Holyoake
And Holyoake looks at the ground,
And there will be more things to say
When the Royal yacht has sailed away.

1963 *1976*

The Axe-Blade

Watching my father sharpen a notched axe-blade
On the lurching grindstone

Worked by a treadle, I liked the whirr that it made
And the way the steel shone

Star-bright when gouts of water played
On the grit, not guessing from the edge's groan

How year by year the lurching world would abrade
Nerve, heart, mind, flesh, bone.

1963 *1976*

Shingle Beach Poem

There is (conveniently) a hollow space
Between the upper and the lower jaws

Of the world serpent. There, as if all days
Were one, the children whack

Their seaweed balls, brag, tussle, comb the shores
For little crabs. There's no road back

To the dream time, and I endure instead
This hunger to be nothing. I supplicate

Dark heaven for the peace of that woman they
Lifted out of the breakers yesterday,

With blue deaf ears, whom Poseidon banged on the kelp-beds
Though she was a good swimmer, her body oatmeal-white

Spotted with shingle. To and fro
She was rolled by the undertow.

This I understand. Sister, remember
Us who wrestle yet in the coil of life's hunger.

1963 1974

East Coast Journey

About twilight we came to the whitewashed pub
On a knuckle of land above the bay

Where a log was riding and the slow
Bird-winged breakers cast up spray.

One of the drinkers round packing cases had
The worn face of a kumara god,

Or so it struck me. Later on
Lying awake in the verandah bedroom

In great dryness of mind I heard the voice of the sea
Reverberating, and thought: As a man

Grows older he does not want beer, bread, or the prancing flesh,
But the arms of the eater of life, Hine-nui-te-po,

With teeth of obsidian and hair like kelp
Flashing and glimmering at the edge of the horizon.

1962–3 1966

Pig Island Letters

to Maurice Shadbolt

1

The gap you speak of – yes, I find it so,
The menopause of the mind. I think of it
As a little death, practising for the greater,
For the undertaker who won't have read
Your stories or my verse –
Or that a self had died
Who handled ideas like bombs,

In that bare southern town
At a party on a cold night
Men seen as ghosts, women like trees walking,
Seen from the floor, a forest of legs and bums
For the climbing boy, the book-bred one.

And this, the moment of art, can never stay.
Wives in the kitchen cease to smile as we go
Into the gap itself, the solid night
Where poor drunks fear the icy firmament:
Man is a walking grave,

That is where I start from. Though often
Where the Leith Stream wandered down
Its culvert, crinkled labia of blossom
On the trees beside the weir
Captured and held the fugitive
From time, from self, from the iron pyramid,

These were diversions. Give my love
To Vic. He is aware of
The albatross. In the Otago storms
Carrying spray to salt the landward farms
The wind is a drunkard. Whoever can listen
Long enough will write again.

21 September 1963 1966

2

From an old house shaded with macrocarpas
Rises my malady.
Love is not valued much in Pig Island
Though we admire its walking parody,

That brisk gaunt woman in the kitchen
Feeding the coal range, sullen
To all strangers, lest one should be
Her antique horn-red Satan.

Her man, much baffled, grousing in the pub,
Discusses sales
Of yearling lambs, the timber in a tree
Thrown down by autumn gales,

Her daughter, reading in her room
A catalogue of dresses,
Can drive a tractor, goes to Training College,
Will vote on the side of the Bosses,

Her son is moodier, has seen
An angel with a sword
Standing above the clump of old man manuka
Just waiting for the word

To overturn the cities and the rivers
And split the house like a rotten totara log.
Quite unconcerned he sets his traps for 'possums
And whistles to his dog.

The man who talks to the masters of Pig Island
About the love they dread
Plaits ropes of sand, yet I was born among them
And will lie some day with their dead.

1963 1966

3

That other Baxter the Sectarian
Said that the bodies of the damned will burn
Like stubble thrown into a red-hot oven
On Judgement Day. In Calvin's town
At seventeen I thought I might see
Not fire but water rise

From the shelves of surf beyond St Clair
To clang the dry bell. Gripping
A pillow wife in bed
I did my convict drill,
And when I made a mother of the keg
The town split open like an owl's egg
Breaking the ladders down. It was
Perhaps the winter of beginning:

Frost standing up like stubble in the streets
Below the knees of Maori Hill,
Looking for the last simplicity
And nothing to explain it in the books,
In a room where the wind clattered the blind-cord
In the bed of a girl with long plaits
I found the point of entry,
The place where father Adam died.

Meanwhile a boy with dog and ferret
Climbed up the gorse track from the sea
To the turn at the top of the gully
Twelve paces past the cabbage tree,
And saw from the crest of the hill
Pillars of rain move on the dark sea,
A cloud of fire rise up above Japan,
God's body blazing on damnation's tree.

Thank you for the letter. I read your book
Five days ago: it has the slow
Imperceptible wingbeat of the hawk
Above the dry scrublands. The kill is there
In the Maori riverbed below
Where bones glitter. I could tell
Of other matters, but not now.

11 October 1963 1966

4

The censor will not let my lines reveal
Pig Island spinning on the potter's wheel.

A skinny wench in jeans with a kea's eye:
The rack on which our modern martyrs die.

I prophesy these young delinquent bags
Will graduate to grim demanding hags.

Our women chiefly carry in their bones
The curse that stuck to the scattered oven stones.

How often Remuera girls abort
Has not been mentioned in the Hunn Report.

Holyoake yammering from a kauri stump —
God save us all! I need a stomach pump.

Sea-eggs, puha, pork, and kumara:
The Maori owned the land. I have a camera.

Though Freud and God may bless the marriage vow
You must know how to work the hillside plough.

The sun is warm, the nosebag smells of hay,
The wind is blowing from the north today.

You who were pulled apart by four draught horses,
Saint Hippolytus, pray for us!

1963 *1966*

5

Long ago, in a ghostly summer,
Somebody held a burning-glass
Above the ants on mountains of crumbed asphalt,
So that one lived, another died:
The hawk's eye, the man in the sky
With his vats of poison cloud
Like Jeyes Fluid. Above the old river
The bridge was a broad mother,
And the small drum of the heart beat loud,

Where the salt gush flowed in
Hooking the fish of Maui on a pin.

To learn the tricks of water
From the boathouse keeper's daughter
Is the task of time. I make
My genuflection at an iron altar
Before the black fish rise, the weather break.

1963 *1966*

6

The hope of the body was coherent love
As if the water sighing on the shores
Would penetrate the hardening muscle, loosen
Whatever had condemned itself in us:
Not the brown flagon, not the lips
Anonymously pressed in the dim light,
But a belief in bodily truth rising
From fountains of Bohemia and the night,

The truth behind the lie behind the truth
That Fairburn told us, gaunt
As the great moa, throwing the twisted blunt
Darts in a pub this side of Puhoi – 'No
Words make up for what we had in youth.'
For what we did not have: that hunger caught
Each of us, and left us burnt,
Split open, grit-dry, sifting the ash of thought.

1963 *1966*

7

This love that heals like a crooked limb
In each of us, source of our grief,
Could tell us if we cared to listen, why
Sons by mayhem, daughters by harlotry
Pluck down the sky's rage on settled houses:
The thin girl and the cornerboy
Whose angers mask their love
Unwind, unwind the bandages
That hide in each the hope of joy.

For me it is the weirs that mention
The love that we destroy
By long evasion, politics and art,
And speech that is a kind of contraception:

A streetlight flashing down
On muscled water, bodies in the shade,
Tears on a moonwhite face, the voice
Of time from the grave of water speaking to
Those who are lucky to be sad.

11 October 1963 1966

8

When I was only semen in a gland
Or less than that, my father hung
From a torture post at Mud Farm
Because he would not kill. The guards
Fried sausages, and as the snow came darkly
I feared a death by cold in the cold groin
And plotted revolution. His black and swollen thumbs
Explained the brotherhood of man,

But he is old now in his apple garden
And we have seen our strong Antaeus die
In the glass castle of the bureaucracies
Robbing our bread of salt. Shall Marx and Christ
Share beds this side of Jordan? I set now
Unwillingly these words down:

Political action in its source is pure,
Human, direct, but in its civil function
Becomes the jail it laboured to destroy.

1963 1966

9

Look at the simple caption of success,
The poet as family man,
Head between thumbs at mass, nailing a trolley,
Letting the tomcat in:

Then turn the hourglass over, find the other
Convict self, incorrigible, scarred
With what the bottle and the sex games taught,
The black triangle, the whips of sin.
The first gets all his meat from the skull-faced twin,
Sharpening a dagger out of a spoon,
Struggling to speak through the gags of a poem:
When both can make a third my work is done.

Nor will the obituary ever indicate
How much we needed friends,
Like Fitz at the National
Speaking of his hydatid cyst,
A football underneath the lung,
Or Lowry in Auckland: all who held the door
And gave us space for art,
Time for the re-shaping of the heart:
Those whom the arrow-makers honour least,
Companions to the manbeast,
One man in many, touching the flayed hide gently,
A brother to the artist and a nurse.

The trees rustle as October comes
And fantails batter on the glass,
Season when the day nurse tuts and hums
Laying out pills and orange juice
For one who walks the bridge of dread
As oedema sets in,
While through the bogs and gullies of Pig Island
Bellies are beaten like skin drums
In pup tents, under flax or lupin shade,

As if the sun were a keg. And this man
On the postman's round will meditate
The horn of Jacob withered at the root
Or quirks of weather. None
Grow old easily. The poem is
A plank laid over the lion's den.

12 October 1963 *1966*

10

To outflank age – a corrugated shack
With fried pauas in the pan,
Beside a bay somewhere, grandchildren in tribes
Wrestling in the long grass, seawater, sleep,
While cloud and green tree like sisters keep
The last door for the natural man.

It will be what it is, half-life,
For the mystery requires
A victim – Marsyas the manbeast
Hung up and flayed on a fir tree,
Or a death by inches, catheter and wife
Troubling an old man's vanity.

11 October 1963 *1966*

11

Tonight I read my son a story
About the bees of Baiame, who tell the east wind
To blow down rain, so that the flowers grow
In dry Australia, and the crow *wirinun*
Who jailed the west wind in a hollow log:

My son who is able to build a tree house
With vine ladders, my son
In his brown knitted jersey and dungarees,
Makes clowns and animals, a world of creatures
To populate paradise,

And when he hands me easily
The key of entry, my joy must be dissembled
Under a shutter of horn, a dark lantern,
In case it should too brightly burn,

Because the journey has begun
Into the land where the sun is silent
And no one may enter the tree house
That hides the bones of a child in the forest of a man.

1963 1966

12

The dark wood Dante wrote of
Is no more than the self, the wandering gulf
That calls itself a man, seen
Through the dark prism of self-love:
Under the leafy screen
Lion, leopard, wolf,
Show by their anger we are not yet slain.

Our loves have tied us to the wheel
From which it is death to be unbound,
Yet unexpected, unpredictable,
Like speckled rain that falls on a wave,
Come the light fingers on the wound,
Or where the marae meets the cattle hill
The face of Beatrice moving in the grove.

1963 1966

13

Stat crux dum volvitur orbis: I will sing
In the whale's belly.
                    'Great Mother of God
Sweeten my foul breath. I wait for a death.
Cradle me, Lady, on the day they carry
My body down the bush track to the road
To the rollers of the decorous van.
The leper's stump, the thick voice of the drunk,
Are knocking at Nazareth. I am a naked man.'

'How can I let you in?
The time for talk has gone;
A mountain is the threshold stone.'

'Mother, I come alone.
No books, no bread
Are left in my swag.'

'Why are your hands not clean?'

'There was no soap in the whole damned town.'

'God's grace has need of man's apology.'

'Your face is my theology.'

'Yes; but I gave you a jewel to bring.'

'In the thick gorse of the gully
I lost your signet ring.'

'Why should I listen then?'

'On Skull Hill there was none,
No scapular, no sign,
Only the words, *I thirst*,
When the blood of a convict burst
From the body of your son.'

'You may come in.'

Is it like that? At least I know no better;
After a night of argument
Mythical, theological, political,
Somebody has the sense to get a boat
And row out towards the crayfish rocks
Where, diving deep, the downward swimmer
Finds fresh water rising up,

A mounded water breast, a fountain,
An invisible tree whose roots cannot be found;

As that wild nymph of water rises
So does the God in man.

13 October 1963 1966

The Waves

1

Accepted here, here only,
For what one is, not the chalk mask,
Gentility of a robot or a clown,
But the sad mandrake torn
From earth, getting no likely truce on earth,
The brat of sighs, less wise than the afterbirth,
The one who should have not perhaps been born.

The wave ignores, consoles, flowing and ebbing
Without reflection. Sand or oven ash
Trickling from the roots of matted swordgrass
Count thirty-seven years between
The sweet first spout of milk and this dried-up
Poem with no breasts, my concubine.

The wave bangs in channels of gnarled stone.

2

The island like an old cleft skull
With tussock and bone needles on its forehead
Lives in the world before the settlers came
With gun and almanac.
One half-mad

Solitary six-foot fisherman
Blasted a passage out with gelignite
Between the shore and the island templebone
To let his boat come in, changing the drift
Of water from the bay.

                        There are veins of gold
In the reef below the sand.

                        I heard
Often, when young, the dialogue
Of wave with wave contending in that gullet
Where now the mussel-pickers go
Safely because the tide is low:
The strangled weight of sex and intellect
Contending and rejected in the cave
Where under weed gates the white octopus
Haunter and waker of the coast
In storms of genesis contains his power.

3

The sound of the sea would enter
That book-lined upper room,
Penetrating the convict dream
Of wordy love, as ropes of semen
Hang useless in the man's groin,
Or the bluebottle husk on the pane
Judged by the spider.

The slow language of the waves
Gave hope of truth to come,
Wideness, a dark meeting
With a woman with a body like the moon,
The mouths of water speaking
Putting aside the barren peace
Of those who are naked only in their graves.

4

At high tide I the burning
Mandrake coffinless stood
And saw the moon stride over
The belly of the flood
Against the tide's turning,
The horned and processional
Goddess of sexual pain
Who kills the mandrake I.
Though every stone and shell
Blazed in the superhuman
Arrows of light that fell
From the double axe and skull,
Lest I should be turned to rock
Or as a serpent glide
Or howl in a wolf's hide,
I called aloud for one
Living and breathing woman
To stand between and cover
My body with her own,
But there was none alive
Between the sea and the rock,
And my own lass who lay
At peace in her deft room,
Being curbed by gentility
Would never rise and run
Down over the black dune
With her grass-green skirt at her knee
To grip the burning ghost,
To lie with the naked man.
That huntress in the sky
Strode on, strode on,
The tide swung back, and I
Under the shade of a green bank stood
With poison crystals whirling in my blood
From the arrow in the breastbone.

5

How to distinguish from the flux of fire,
Salt tides and air, some ruler
Other than octopus, man–killing moon
Or our own twist of thought, breeds pain.
Wings of the albatross whose shadow
Lies on the seas at noon

I take as the type of a spirit bent
By abstract solitude,
Accepting all. The waves do not debase
Or drown what shares their fluid motion,
Yet hard for human blood

Is the habit of relinquishment,
Abandoning of Isaac to the knife
That tortured Abraham. Come now;
Poems are trash, the flesh I love will die,
Desire is bafflement,
But one may say that father Noah kept
Watch while the wild beasts slept,

Not knowing even if land would rise
Out of the barren waves.
That ark I keep, that watch on the edge of sleep,
While the dark water heaves.

1963 *1969*

Letter to Robert Burns

King Robert, on your anvil stone
Above the lumbering Octagon,
To you I raise a brother's horn
Led by the wandering unicorn
Of total insecurity.
Never let your dead eye look
Up from Highland Mary's book
To the fat scrag-end of the Varsity.
Kilmarnock hag and dominie
Watch there the grey Leith water drum
With laughter from a bird's beak
At what their learning has left out.
They tried to make my devil speak
With the iron boot of education
(Psychology, French, Latin) –
But though they drove the wedges in
Till the blood and marrow spouted out,
That spirit was dumb.

Robert, only a heart I bring,
No gold of words to grace a king,
Nor can a stranger lift that flail
That cracked the wall of Calvin's jail
And earned you the lead garland of
A people's moralizing love,
Till any Scotsman with the shakes
Can pile on your head his mistakes
And petrify a boozaroo
Reciting *Tam o' Shanter* through;
And there's an old black frost that freezes
Apollo's balls and the blood of Jesus
In this dry, narrow-gutted town.
Often enough I stumbled down
From Maori Hill to the railway station
(When Aussie gin was half the price)
Making my Easter meditation

In the wilderness of fire and ice
Where a Puritan gets his orientation.

King Robert with the horn of stone!
Perhaps your handcuffs were my own;
Your coffin-cradle was the blank
Medusa conscience of a drunk
That hankers for the purity
Of an imagined infancy,
And after riding seven whores
Approaches God upon all fours,
Crying, 'O thou great Incubus,
Help me or turn me to a walrus!'
And in hangover weeps to see
A playing child or a walnut tree.
If, lying in the pub latrine,
You muttered, 'Take me back to Jean,'
The reason for your mandrake groans
Is wrapped like wire around my bones.

Not too far from the Leith water
My mother saw the mandrake grow
And pulled it. A professor's daughter,
She told me some time after how
She had been frightened by a cow
So that the birth-sac broke too soon
And on the twenty-ninth of June
Prematurely I looked at the walls
And yelled. The Plunket nurse ran in
To scissor off my valued foreskin,
But one thing staggered that grimalkin:
Poets are born with three balls.

Biology, mythology,
Go underground when the bookmen preach,
And I must thank the lass who taught me
My catechism at Tunnel Beach;
For when the hogmagandie ended
And I lay thunder-struck and winded,

The snake-haired Muse came out of the sky
And showed her double axe to me.
Since then I die and do not die.
'Jimmy,' she said, 'you are my ugliest son;
I'll break you like a herring-bone.'

I fill my pipe with black tobacco
And watch a dead man's ember glow.

1963 *1967*

Tomcat

This tomcat cuts across the
zones of the respectable
through fences, walls, following
other routes, his own. I see
the sad whiskered skull-mouth fall
wide, complainingly, asking

to be picked up and fed, when
I thump up the steps through bush
at 4 p.m. He has no
dignity, thank God! has grown
older, scruffier, the ash–
black coat sporting one or two

flowers like round stars, badges
of bouts and fights. The snake head
is seamed on top with rough scars:
old Samurai! He lodges
in cellars, and the tight furred
scrotum drives him into wars

as if mad, yet tumbling on
the rug looks female, Turkish-
trousered. His bagpipe shriek at
sluggish dawn dragged me out in
pyiamas to comb the bush
(he being under the vet

for septic bites): the old fool
stood, body hard as a board,
heart thudding, hair on end, at
the house corner, terrible,
yelling at something. They said,
'Get him doctored.' I think not.

1960–4 *1966*

from *The Holy Life and Death of Concrete Grady*

1   The Ballad of Grady's Dream

One clink black night in June
Concrete Grady sat
Between the knees of the pines
With Old Jack Flynn his mate,

And through the harbour fog
The guts of Wellington
Glowed like a great morgue
Where even the cops had gone.

'I had a dream,' said Grady –
Flynn said, 'Stuff your dream!
I'd give my ballocks now
For a bucket of steam.'

'I had a dream,' said Grady,
'When I slept in Mulligan's woodyard
Under a wad of roofing iron;
I was a white bird,

'And then a gale caught me
And threw me north;
There was nothing left standing
On the bare-arsed earth,

'And I thought of the time in Crete
When we jammed the Bren gun
And the paratroops came over
Like washing on a line,

'And you'll remember, Jack,
Because you were there,
We shot twelve prisoners
In Imvros village square;

'Because the wind blew me
To the door of a stone barn,
And the Nazi lads were sitting
At a table playing cards –

'*Sergeant, come in*, they said,
We've kept you a place –
And when they turned I saw
The red-hot bone in each one's face,

'So I let the wind carry
Me out past Kapiti
In the belly of the storm above
A thousand miles of sea,

'Till I came to a blind cliff
That got no sun,
Deep as the cunning of Hell
And high as the trouble of man.

'There was one gap in it
Where only a bird could fly;
I said the Hail Mary
And threaded the needle's eye,

'And there in a green garden
I saw the Tramways Band
And a crowd of people walking
With flagons in their hands,

'And on a bullock wagon
The Host Itself with seven nuns,
And one of them had the face
Of Rose O'Rourke when she was young.'

'You've struck it there,' said Flynn,
'She'd be a bit of all right;
But I'd give old Rose the go-by
For a bottle of steam tonight.'

1965 *1966*

Thoughts of a Remuera Housewife

The tranquillizers on my
glass-topped table, black-and-green
pomegranate seeds, belong to
Pluto, that rough king – so I
have eaten six, to go in
quietly, quietly through

the dark mirror to his world
of chaos and the grave – 'Ann,
how strong you are!' my mother
said yesterday when the wild
pony all but threw Robin
under its hooves; I got her

to mount again. They don't know
I am Pluto's Queen ... Oh yes,
I kept your letter saying
it was no good – what did you
mean by that? The drugged clouds race
over the gun-pit facing

all storm, where you stopped the car
and undid my jersey – now
my husband is undressing
and jerking at his collar
with the Bugs Bunny grin I
hated so ... Our sort of dying

kept me young – my love, how high
the cocksfoot was! our own bed
walled in by soldier stalks of
grass – no one else could touch me,
among the lions' dens – mad,
happy, lost! In Pluto's cave

from granite thrones we watch the
ghosts whirling like snaking fog
quietly, quietly down
to their own urn, not to see
ever the sun's sweat-streaked flag
thunder again ... In London

do they play Schubert or Brahms
in asbestos rooms? Do girls
bite your throat? When you turned me
into a violin (dreams
are what I go by) that pulse
in your neck ... My Satan, why

did you not stay where flames rise
always up? You said no one
can fight the world ... No; it's not
a world at all, but Pluto's
iron-black star, the quiet
planet furthest from the sun.

1962–5 *1966*

To a Print of Queen Victoria

I advise rest; the farmhouse
we dug you up in has been
modernized, and the people
who hung you as their ikon
against the long passage wall
are underground – Incubus

and excellent woman, we
inherit the bone acre
of your cages and laws. This
dull green land suckled at your
blood's *frigor Anglicanus*,
crowning with a housewife's tally

the void of Empire, does not
remember you – and certain
bloody bandaged ghosts rising
from holes of Armageddon
at Gallipoli or Sling
Camp, would like to fire a shot

through the gilt frame. I advise
rest, Madam; and yet the tomb
holds much that we must travel
barely without. Your print – 'from
an original pencil
drawing by the Marchioness

'of Granby, March, eighteen nine-
ty seven ...' Little mouth, strong
nose and hooded eye – they speak
of half-truths my type have slung
out of the window, and lack
and feel the lack too late. Queen,

you stand most for the time of
early light, clay roads, great trees
unfelled, and the smoke from huts
where girls in sack dresses
stole butter ... The small rain spits
today. You smile in your grave.

1951–65 *1966*

Ballad of Nine Jobs

At Purakanui I buried my shadow
Under the edge of a hillside plough.

At Wanaka I rode a stumble-
Footed pony without a saddle.

At the Burnside works I still stank
Of dead sheep, sober or drunk.

At Green Island I watched the iron
Burst from the rolls like a red-hot dragon.

On Cashmere Hills in the TB wards
I smuggled booze and scrubbed the morgue.

At Epuni with a buttoned fly
I taught the children how to lie.

In Wellington I did it hard
Carving stones in Caesar's graveyard.

Now I carry a postman's bag
In Wadestown through the grit and fog.

All the time inside my scone
I peel away the onion skin
Till the earth talks through the man.

1965 *1976*

A Bucket of Blood for a Dollar

a conversation between Uncle Sam and the Rt. Hon. Keith Holyoake, Prime Minister of New Zealand

'You'll have to learn,' said Uncle Sam,
'The Yankee way of work
Now that you've joined in our crusade
Against the modern Turk;
The capital of the Commonwealth is
Not London, but New York.'

'Don't tell them that,' cried Holyoake,
'In Thames or Dannevirke.'

'Then use your loaf,' said Uncle Sam,
'Newspapers hit the eye;
If you get trouble from the men
That you can't bluff or buy,
Just spread the word that they're all Reds
And let the rumours fly.'

'I'll bang the drum,' said Holyoake –
And yet he heaved a sigh.

'Tell them straight,' said Uncle Sam,
'That it's a dirty war;
Mention the Freedom of the West
That we are fighting for;
But keep the money side of it
Well tucked behind the door.'

'I'll make it sound,' said Holyoake,
'Just like a football score.'

'Between the fights,' said Uncle Sam,
'They'll need some exercise;
There's a thousand brothels in Saigon
Where they can fraternize.
The peasants send their daughters there
When they have no rice.'

'Let's not be coarse,' said Holyoake,
Turning up his eyes.

'I fried a village,' said Uncle Sam,
'With the new phosphorus bomb
The day a Yankee Army nurse
Was killed by the Viet Cong;
A white dame's worth a million gooks –
In Asia, *we* belong.'

'Your chivalry,' said Holyoake,
'Puts angels in the wrong.'

'The newest way,' said Uncle Sam,
'To interrogate the brutes
Is a wet wire on the private parts
That half-electrocutes –
Though I do hate having to wash
Their vomit from my boots.'

'Don't talk so loud!' groaned Holyoake –
'We'll want the churches' votes.'

'I'm a simple chap,' sighed Holyoake,
'Politics hurt my head;
But why do you scrap with China
To the tune of a million dead
And sign a Pact with Russia,
When both of them are Red?'

'Get with it, Keith,' said Uncle Sam,
'We need the East for trade.'

'I'm a simple chap,' said Holyoake,
'Politics frighten me;
But whether it's frozen meat or men
We send across the sea,
We want good prices for our veal –
What can you guarantee?'

'Just name your price,' said Uncle Sam,
'And leave the rest to me.'

1965 *1965*

The Old Earth Closet

a tribute to regional poetry

Oh some will sing of Dannevirke
And some will sing of Troy
And some of girls on Lambton Quay.
But since I was a boy
A genuine earth closet
Is my peculiar joy.

The one my Grandad dug when first
He reached this island shore
Was sunk into volcanic rock
For thirty feet or more –
He kept the family Bible
Nailed up behind the door.

From Genesis to Amos
He had travelled ere he died
(A frugal Scottish farmer
Whose potatoes were his pride)
And they laid its tattered pages
In the coffin by his side.

The old earth dyke was standing
In my father's day and mine
With its seat of polished hardwood
And its door of knotted pine –
To a faithless generation
It remaineth as a sign.

And to that seat of refuge
In my boyhood I would come
To meditate for hours and hear
Aeolian voices drum
In the cave of the Delphic oracle,
Till my backside was numb.

There in the drowsy summer light
My first bad verse was made,
My first experiments in Yoga
Conducted in its shade –
May none disturb that hallowed spot
With an unreverent spade!

Across the hills of manuka
I watched the cows come home,
And as they wandered up the track
It turned my heart to stone
That I was a New Zealander
And therefore Man Alone.

And that is why my verses plod
So deep in our native clay –
To regional environment
This tribute I must pay
Lest an earth closet swallow me
Upon the Judgement Day.

1954–65 *1965*

The Lion Skin

The old man with a yellow flower on his coat
Came to my office, climbing twenty-eight steps,
With a strong smell of death about his person
From the caves of the underworld.
The receptionist was troubled by his breath
Understandably.
                          Not every morning tea break
Does Baron Saturday visit his parishioners
Walking stiffly, strutting almost,
With a cigar in his teeth – she might have remembered
Lying awake as if nailed by a spear
Two nights ago, with the void of her life
Glassed in a dark window – but suitably enough
She preferred to forget it.
                          I welcomed him
And poured him a glass of cherry brandy,
Talked with him for half an hour or so,
Having need of his strength, the skin of a dead lion,
In the town whose ladders are made of coffin wood.

The flower on his coat blazed like a dark sun.

1965 *1967*

On Possessing the Burns Fellowship 1966

to Nicholas Zissermann

Trees move slowly. The rain drops arrows
As on the Spartans from the Persian bowstring
Some while ago, across the tennis court
Behind the convent they hope to pull down,

And I who wrote in '62,
Dear ghosts, let me abandon
What cannot be held against
Hangmen and educators, the city of youth! —

Drink fresh percolated coffee, lounging
In the new house, at the flash red kitchen table,
A Varsity person, with an office
Just round the corner — what nonsense!

If there is any culture here
It comes from the black south wind
Howling above the factories
A handsbreadth from Antarctica,

Whatever the architect and planner
Least understand — not impossibly the voice
Of an oracle rising from that
Old battered green verandah

Beyond the board fence: a blood transfusion
From the earth's thick veins! As if
Caesar had died, and clouds, leaves, conspired to make
A dark mocking funeral wreath.

1962–6 1967

At Aramoana

Boulders interrupt the long
jetty from whose black asphalt
tongue the godwits fly to their
Siberian lakes, or – *Abba,*
father! – melt like ash or salt
in the void white thundering

wilderness. Yet on the spit
sheaves of water bow as if
to the sickle, and boys make
from earth, air, a goatskin ark,
each watching the same girl of
blood and fibreglass go out

into the surf and shake back
the hanging gardens of her
sun-bleached hair. I turn also
to my dream, in nooks below
the sandhill cone, where Gea
speaks in parables of rock,

wordless, unconnected with
the acedia of a tribe
never *once* happy, never
at peace ... There is no other
rest for the heart, but these drab
mats of cutty-grass, no truth

outside her changing and austere
testament of sand. Beyond
her breast, though, I must walk on
to where the black swells begin
Abba, father – to swamp, pound
and hurt the land – on further,

where the serpent current flows
out of the harbour gates, long-
flowing, strongly tugging at
the roots of the world. The night
sky tells that after singing
silence is the only voice.

1966 *1967*

The Maori Jesus

I saw the Maori Jesus
Walking on Wellington Harbour.
He wore blue dungarees.
His beard and hair were long.
His breath smelt of mussels and paraoa.
When he smiled it looked like the dawn.
When he broke wind the little fishes trembled.
When he frowned the ground shook.
When he laughed everybody got drunk.

The Maori Jesus came on shore
And picked out his twelve disciples.
One cleaned toilets in the Railway Station;
His hands were scrubbed red to get the shit out of the pores.
One was a call-girl who turned it up for nothing.
One was a housewife who'd forgotten the Pill
And stuck her TV set in the rubbish can.
One was a little office clerk
Who'd tried to set fire to the Government Buildings.
Yes, and there were several others;
One was an old sad quean;
One was an alcoholic priest
Going slowly mad in a respectable parish.

The Maori Jesus said, 'Man,
From now on the sun will shine.'

He did no miracles;
He played the guitar sitting on the ground.

The first day he was arrested
For having no lawful means of support.
The second day he was beaten up by the cops
For telling a dee his house was not in order.
The third day he was charged with being a Maori
And given a month in Mount Crawford.
The fourth day he was sent to Porirua
For telling a screw the sun would stop rising.
The fifth day lasted seven years
While he worked in the asylum laundry
Never out of the steam.
The sixth day he told the head doctor,
'I am the Light in the Void;
I am who I am.'
The seventh day he was lobotomized;
The brain of God was cut in half.

On the eighth day the sun did not rise.
It didn't rise the day after.
God was neither alive nor dead.
The darkness of the Void,
Mountainous, mile-deep, civilized darkness
Sat on the earth from then till now.

1966 *1979*

Daughter

Daughter, when you were five
I was your Monster;
Leaving the pub, less than half-alive,
Hurtling in a taxi to the Play Centre –

You'd ride like a jockey up Messines Road,
Thumbs in my eyes, your bulky legs
On each side of my booze-filled head –
A red-suited penguin!

I'd spoon you out dollops of mushroom soup,
Peel off the penguin skin, and tuck you down,
Uncap a bottle of White Horse, dredge up
My hangman cobbers from the town …

Five years later I'd wake at 2 a.m.
And see an upright ghost in a nightie
Standing beside my bed, mumbling
About a bad dream it had had –

You'd settle in with me like a bear cub
And wrap your arms halfway round my chest –
An atomic blast set off in the Sahara
Of my schizoid, never-quiet mind!

Incest? The quacks don't know their job.
I was your father,
I treated you like bone china,
Sent you sleepwalking back to your cot.

At seventeen your face is powder-white,
Your hair is a black dyed fountain,
Mooching round the house you slam doors
And wait to be rung up.

Why won't you work? That boil on your heel
Comes from going barefoot
In the wet streets. Last night
I dreamt I burnt a fish-skin coat

To turn you back into a human shape –
Wouldn't you yell! Yet I was glad
When you hoisted your private flag
Against the bourgeois gastanks – You're *my* daughter!

When I go in to wake you up
On a morning of ice and boredom,
You sleep with your mouth open
Like a soldier struck down in battle,

And I'm Narcissus bending over
The water face! From the edge of the pillow,
Red-veined, grape-black,
My own eye looks back.

1966 *1973*

from *Words to Lay a Strong Ghost*

after Catullus

1   The Party

A kind of cave – still on the brandy,
And coming in from outside,
I didn't like it – the room like a tunnel
And everybody gassing in chairs –

Or count on finding you there, smiling
Like a stone Diana at
Egnatius' horse-laugh – not my business exactly
That he cleans his teeth with AJAX,

But he's the ugliest South Island con man
Who ever beat up a cripple ...
Maleesh – the booze rolls back, madam;
I'm stuck here in the void

Looking at my journey's end –
Two breasts like towers – the same face
That brought Troy crashing
Down like a chicken coop – black wood and flames!

1966 *1973*

12   The Rock

Arms of Promethean rock
Thrust out on either
Side of a bare white strip
Of wave-ridged sand – long before

I ever met you, Pyrrha,
The free world held me in its heart,
And half my grief is only
The grief of a child torn from the breast

Who remembers – who cannot forget
The shielding arms of a father,
Maybe Poseidon – out there
Where the waves never cease to break

In the calmest weather, there's a hump-backed
Jut of reef – we called it Lion Rock –
Growling with its wild white mane
As if it told us even then

Death is the one door out of the labyrinth!
Not your fault – to love, hate, die,
Is natural – as under quick sand-grains
The broken bladders lie.

1966 *1973*

13   The Flower

They've bricked up the arch, Pyrrha,
That used to lead into
Your flat on Castle Street – Lord, how
I'd pound the kerb for hours,

Turning this way and that
Outside it, like a hooked fish
Wanting the bait but not the barb –
Or else a magnetized needle!

Well; they've bricked it up – fair
Enough! You've sunk your roots in Australia,
And I'm free to write verses,
Grow old, be married, watch my children clutter

Their lives up … It was always a tomb,
That place of yours! I didn't know
Then how short life is – how few
The ones who really touch us

Right at the quick – I'm a successful
Man of letters, Pyrrha –
Utterly stupid! – a forty-year-old baby
Crying out for a lost nurse

Who never cared much. The principle
That should have made me tick went early
Half underground, as at the paddock's edge
You'll see in autumn some flower

(Let's say a dandelion)
Go under the farmer's boots
Like a faded sun
Cut with a spade.

1966 *1973*

To my Father in Spring

Father, the fishermen go
down to the rocks at twilight
when earth in the undertow

of silence is drowning, yet
they tread the bladdered weedbeds
as if death and life were but

the variation of tides –
while you in your garden shift
carefully the broken sods

to prop the daffodils left
after spring hail. You carry
a kerosene tin of soft

bread and mutton bones to the
jumping hens that lay their eggs
under the bushes slily –

not always firm on your legs
at eighty-four. Well, father,
in a world of bombs and drugs

you charm me still – no other
man is quite like you! That smile
like a low sun on water

tells of a cross to come. Shall
I eavesdrop when Job cries out
to the Rock of Israel?

No; but mourn the fishing net
hung up to dry, and walk with
you the short track to the gate

where crocuses lift the earth.

1966 *1973*

Travelling to Dunedin

We ride south on a Wednesday
Into the clearer weather,

Gently packed like foetuses in the dead
Belly of the thunderbird,

Down to the city of our youth
(My wife and I) – it's a quiet place;

But the pattern shifts a little. Those houses on Lookout Point
(Skull-grey as something painted by Utrillo)

Ambiguously glitter. We notice now
That a quarry like a cancer

Has cut away half of the smaller breast
Of Saddle Hill. And I remember

How in these parts the dead sleep
Under rough clay, who will rise up

In rage and hope at the Judgement Day,
Denying the quiet town, the quiet clouds,

Their hard, sod-cutting hands, so like our own,
Bent in the cramp of lifelong separate pain.

1966 *1974*

At Queenstown

If you go up on a clear dry morning
You may find a few dog tracks in the frozen slush

Of the steep road, and round the next bend
The fir trees with their pollen-bearing candles,

Then at the top of the long hill
A chalet, not a monastery,

From which one looks down at the view:
The boats like water beetles,

Wooden motels and pine tree islands ...
And later a full moon will take

Her own photograph of the Remarkables,
Black rock veined with August snow!

Now as the blind eye
In your brain struggles to open,

Admit: It's nice, but not quite human,
A dipsomaniac's limbo,

To sit like a sack of shit in a smart bar,
Never out of the death trance, looking at

The faceless terraced hills, the enormous blue
Vacant eyeball of the lake

That won't notice whether you go or stay
But only whether you have the money.

1966 *1976*

At the Fox Glacier Hotel

One kind of love, a Tourist Bureau print
Of the Alps reflected in Lake Matheson

(Turned upside down it would look the same)
Smiles in the dining room, a lovely mirror

For any middle-aged Narcissus to drown in –
I'm peculiar; I don't want to fall upwards

Into the sky! Now, as the red-eyed tough
West Coast beer-drinkers climb into their trucks

And roar off between colonnades
Of mossed rimu, I sit for a while in the lounge

In front of a fire of end planks
And wait for bedtime with my wife and son,

Thinking about the huge ice torrent moving
Over bluffs and bowls of rock (some other

Kind of love) at the top of the valley –
How it might crack our public looking-glass

If it came down to us, jumping
A century in twenty minutes,

So that we saw, out of the same window
Upstairs where my underpants are hanging to dry,

Suddenly – no, not ourselves
Reflected, or a yellow petrol hoarding,

But the other love, yearning over our roofs
Black pinnacles and fangs of toppling ice.

1966 *1973*

Mother and Son

1

Blowflies dive-bomb the sitting-room
Table, this dry spring morning,

In my mother's house. As I did in my 'teens,
I listen again to the Roman-lettered clock

Chiming beside the statue of Ghandi
Striding towards God without any shadow

Along the mantelpiece. Time is a spokeless wheel.
Fantails have built a nest on the warm house wall

Among the passion-vines. The male one lurks.
The female spreads her fan. Out in the rock garden

White-headed my mother weeds red polyanthus,
Anemone, Andean crocus,

And the gold and pearl trumpets called angels' tears.
Mother, I can't ever wholly belong

In your world. What if the dancing fantail
Should hatch tomorrow a dragon's egg?

Mother, in all our truces of the heart
I hear the pearl-white angels musically weeping.

2

There's more to it. Those wood-framed photographs
Also beside the clock, contain your doubtful angels,

My brother with hair diagonally brushed
Over his forehead, with a hot dark eye,

And myself, the baby blondish drowsing child
So very slow to move away from the womb!

Saddled and ridden to Iceland and back by the night-hag
He learnt early that prayers don't work, or work

After the need has gone. Mother, your son
Had gained a pass degree in Demonology

Before he was twelve – how else can you make a poet? –
Yet we're at one in the Catholic Church.

I go out to meet you. Someone is burning weeds
Next door. The mother fantail flutters

Chirping with white eyebrows and white throat
On a branch of lawsoniana, and the darting

Father bird comes close when I whisper to him
With a susurrus of the tongue.

1966 *1973*

At Kuri Bush

A few days back I climbed the mound
Where the farmhouse had stood,

As green as any that the Maoris made
Along that coast. The fog was blowing

Through gates and up gullies
Hiding even the stems of cocksfoot grass

That had sprung up in place of
The sitting-room table and the small brass

Kerosene lamp my mother lighted
Every night, whose white wick would burn

Without changing colour. Somebody must have
Used the old brushwood fence for kindling

Twenty years ago. Outside it
My father stood when I was three or less,

Holding me up to look at
The gigantic rotating wheel of the stars

Whose time isn't ours. The mound yielded
No bones, no coins, but only

A chip of the fallen chimney
I put in the pocket of a damp coat

Before I bumbled back down to the road
With soaking trousers. That splinter of slate

Rubbed by keys and cloth like an amulet
Would hold me back if I tried to leave this island

For the streets of London or New York.
I hope one day they'll plant me in

The kind of hole they dig for horses
Under a hilltop cabbage tree

Not too far from the river that goes
Southwards to the always talking sea.

1966 *1973*

At Brighton Bay

Two concrete pillars whittled by the tide
Regard the meeting of the bay and river,

Useless as some authority
Whose function is evaded by the water

That flows in wandering channels. I'd go down
In winter, when rain spattered on the wide

Corrugated levels, my body not
My own, but gutted by

The opposites of sex and pain,
Like new-cut banks the river had gouged out

For me to kick down ritually –
That grotesque adolescent fury

We never grow beyond! Today I hoisted myself
Up the rock stair that's called Jacob's Ladder

This end of the bay, shoving through gorse, and stood
On the smooth edge of the flax-covered cliff

That tempted me to suicide
In those times. No squid-armed Venus rose

Out of the surf, but through the smashed gate
Of many winters, from the hurdling water

Came to my heart the invisible spirit
These words have given shape to.

1966 *1976*

Fitz Drives Home the Spigot

When you hammered the spigot in, Fitz,
With blow after blow of a mallet,
I felt the town shudder, very much afraid
That the drunk man would be king,

That the meticulous sorrow
Of widows and spinsters with small zip purses
Would be disregarded by drunken coalmen
Pissing against the hedge,

That daughters would go down singing in droves
To the oil tankers and open their white legs
To rough-handed rum-fed sailors, that well-bred sons
Would dive in your great barrel and happily drown,

That the black bones of Dionysus
Buried under the Fire Assurance Building
Had sprouted a million wild green vines
Cracking the pavements and the gravestones –

But fortunately you did not strike too hard!
The town shook once, and then regained its proper
Monotonous man-killing identity,
While you rubbed your belly and drank one pony beer.

1966 *1967*

Winter River

Nothing is colder than this water in winter
when winds crack the lopped pines
on the Domain bank and send cones
rolling down to the water ...

Thick bare brown roots tangled
below the sod wall. The boys
and their girls would sit on Saturdays
in a fog of awkwardness and watch

the river run out to the bay.
Ah well – it's easy
to come back, more or less alive
inside one's own unbreakable

glass dome, a dying Martian,
and think about youth.
I never liked it much.
I did not venture

to touch the thick blonde matted curls
of those man-swallowing dolls, our big sisters.
I had no sister.
Their giggles made me tremble

and coast away to the bathing shed latrine
in itchy summer torpor,
furiously inventing a unicorn
who hated the metal of Venus.

Yet they weren't metal. Now
they sag on porches, in back rooms,
flabby as I am, and the river
carries a freight of floating pine cones.

1966 *1973*

Grandfather

Old and
bald–headed as a turtle,
I remember you,
grandfather, at the trembling kitchen range –

(all your hopes drawn in
to a pond where the light
flickered and gripped you from above,
your dead wife's love) –

so hot with the damper out
a match would flare
at a touch of its explosive tip
on the black glossy surface!

Ah yes – you'd take
the white bone chanter
down from its rack, finger it and play it
so sweetly, lightly, the wristbone of a man

hollow at each end, or so
I think of it, life measured
into a tube wound round
with bands of silver.

You'd caught the notes, you'd stolen them
long ago, sitting like a young
ferret in a flaxbush while your father
tried to teach the elder son.

He taught you then. A champion piper
you could never read a note,
you *were* the tune! It didn't
help you much

when the bailiffs were in,
and the butcher of God's Word
dragged you in half, much later,
so that you gave up smoking and whisky,

fell, rose, fell, rose, fell,
always a worry to your wife –
my looking-glass twin,
when the fumes were boiling in your head

on a black morning, the horses stamping
unfed, the manuka dripping
in gullies mortgaged to the hilt,
did you say '*I* am Hell'?

I salute whatever
burns, our brother Lucifer
raging! This I understand.
Never the unhurt quiet end.

1967 *1976*

Iron Scythe Song

An appearance of control
Is what the waves could drown;
Seawater like the soul
Is ownable by no one
Though safe enough to watch,
And as I barge through each

White haggard tumbling top
The cold surf bangs my head,
And quickly I go up
To change in the bathing shed,
Leaving my wife and son
To plunge alone,

Then fat and fortyish
With a king-sized ice cream
Snug in its cone, I splash
Through the warm creek and come
Up the road's stony edge
To my father's hawthorn hedge ...

'The scarlet hawthorn flowers
Flaring and fragrant stand,
Land bird and sea bird bears
Hope of new sea and land' –
If the words are callow
I made them long ago,

But while the wind moves
Behind his hat today
The green glittering leaves,
My father lifts and shows me,
Still usable, though rusted,
The scythe his father lifted,

And like the iron scythe
That hangs out of the rain,
By sharpener and by wrath
Worn down to its backbone,
My life has the shape
That it will keep.

1967 *1973*

The River

My brother started the boat engine
Tugging on a cord, and I steered

Upriver with the tide behind us
Close to the outlet of the gorge:

No problem, except when somebody's
Plastic leggings, floating under water,

Twisted round the propellor. That same afternoon,
Lying down flat after lunch, I heard

The river water slapping, and thought about
Three buried selves: child, adolescent,

The young unhappy married man
Who would have hated this place – ah well,

Space is what I love! The three selves dance
In the great eddy below the Taieri bridge,

And I am glad to leave them, sprinkling water
Over the embers that heated the Thermette,

Having at last interpreted the speech
Of the river – 'Does it matter? Does it matter?' –

And carrying like salt and fresh inside me
The opposing currents of my life and death.

1967 1974

At Naseby

'Mountains are mothers' – I wrote
those three words in an MS.
book, beside a new poem,
long ago with a pen cut
from a rooster feather, when
the earth and I were much less

compatible – living then
in a lean-to at the side
of a sun-dried-brick cottage
a yard or two up the road
where they've put a FOR SALE sign –
no bigger than a garage,

but it's the place that counts – I
must have been mad! There are no
mountains here; just the poplars
raining down orange leaves to
rot in ditches, and a spry
shop that sells bread, potatoes,

chutney, magazines – far off
on the skyline a small spoor
of hills, but nearer at hand
nothing apart from the moth-
bright family baches and
sod houses worn by weather

shapeless as graves, among which
water-courses ramble like
veins of memory. I'm not
haunted much, climbing the track
to the swimming-dam, by that
grim boy step by step at watch,

my judge below the larches,
his mind like a coiled spring wound
tight by dread and hope, a quill
tucked in his pocket – because
I have forgotten his wound,
and trudging towards nightfall

I find that whatever is
other than self sleeps now like
a wife at my elbow, with
rough breasts of stone, from whose kiss
I turn, so as not to break
the hymen of Sister Death.

1967 *1976*

Reflections at Lowburn Ferry

They take trucks on board for the river crossing.
Not always safe. It has been known to happen
That the ferry tipped and the truck slid back
Slowly into the Clutha with ten men cursing
And three men praying that the stuck
Cab door would shift. But the willows are green
Low down on the water. I've often thought that when
I finally flake, or a minute after, the gate will open
On this damned ferry. Very likely they won't have heard
Of Good Pope John. They will ask me why
I have no obol under my tongue,
Or a cent, or a penny – unless the price has risen –
And I will float in the mud like an old sad turd,
Never to live, never to die,
Wishing to Christ that Christ would come along,
Even the Protestant Christ, like Oscar Wilde when young,
To shake a tambourine with the souls in prison.

1967 *1974*

Air Flight North

I do not like this chariot. It gives me
Faustian dreams. Undoing the seat belt

And lighting up a smoke, I am able to gaze at
Cattle like maggots on

Green porcelain paddocks, till the loops of the Taieri
Give way to a Christmas tree land

Of firs gripping the brown animal fell
Of hills (like what Nils Holgerssen flew over

On the back of a barnyard goose) – and somewhere
To the right down there, close to the tidal mudflats

(May they keep the peace) my wife and my two children
Do this and that in Cumberland Street.

Now the steel hawk is turning towards
That pale blue monster, the undrinkable ocean.

My mother Gea below me is undressed
Showing her stretchmarks got by long childbearing.

One should not look. Above clouds like ice floes
We drift on. I meditate the doom

Of Icarus, while the hostess brings
Coffee in trim red mugs. A calm flight.

1967 *1974*

Winter Poem to my Wife

Because the fog is a curtain over the town
Because the lights are rare and few like virgins
Because the fire spits little sparks and weeps white resin,
Because I am a wooden husband,

You go away from me down to the roots of water
To find the spiny sea–egg
Whose yolk breaks molten in the mouth,
You go down to the sea gate
And gather the black pods of iron flax!

Because the trees are fur on an old hairy cat
Because the cars travel with windmills in their bellies
Because the houses are shaking their crumbling fists of mildew,
Because I am a warty husband,

You go away from me into the Maori church
To find an old bone flute
Playing by itself in the darkest corner
And the shark's tooth and the flounder
And the tears of the albatross!

I accept these journeys.

Because the wind has lost its powder keg
Because the frost has started to scythe the street
Because the moon is a blind wet crystal,
Because I am a silent husband,

You go away from me to the middle of the bush
To find a coat of stones and staples
Or the lifted hair of the hurricane
That tries to spin the sun in a new direction.
That's not a bad idea.

I accept my fate.

1967 *1974*

Safety

To undo the inside trouser button
And sit on a wooden lavatory
Watching birds – an ethical occupation
Though once it was not so,

The belt undone, the man in his hot skin
Entering what he should not enter,
A woman, a door, a gap in the high stone wall
That constitutes life – let us suppose,

In charity, too drunk to remember it,
Among tangled creepers at the party's end!
Now let God be glad, or sad, who made the creature
And gave him that great sack of guts,

For he is decorous now, concentrating
On cold draughts, bills, wet feet, his bowel motion,
Or anything safe – this old wattled Adam
Back in the garden; behind the safe stone gate.

1967 *1972*

A Small Ode on Mixed Flatting

Elicited by the decision of the Otago University authorities to forbid this practice among students

Dunedin nights are often cold
(I notice it as I grow old);
The south wind scourging from the Pole
Drives every rat to his own hole,
Lashing the drunks who wear thin shirts
And little girls in mini-skirts.
Leander, that Greek lad, was bold
To swim the Hellespont raging cold
To visit Hero in her tower
Just for an amorous half-hour,
And lay his wet brine-tangled head
Upon her pillow – Hush! The dead
Can get good housing – Thomas Bracken,
Smellie, McLeod, McColl, McCracken,
A thousand founding fathers lie
Well roofed against the howling sky
In mixed accommodation – Hush!
It is the living make us blush
Because the young have wicked hearts
And blood to swell their private parts.
To think of corpses pleases me;
They keep such perfect chastity.
O Dr Williams, you were right
To shove the lovers out of sight;
Now they can wander half the night
Through coffee house and street and park
And fidget in the dripping dark,
While we play Mozart and applaud
The angel with the flaming sword!
King Calvin in his grave will smile
To know we know that man is vile;
But Robert Burns, that sad old rip
From whom I got my Fellowship

Will grunt upon his rain-washed stone
Above the empty Octagon,
And say – 'O that I had the strength
To slip yon lassie half a length!
Apollo! Venus! Bless my ballocks!
Where are the games, the hugs, the frolics?
Are all you bastards melancholics?
Have you forgotten that your city
Was founded well in bastardry
And half your elders (God be thankit)
Were born the wrong side of the blanket?
You scholars, throw away your books
And learn your songs from lasses' looks
As I did once – ' Ah, well; it's grim;
But I will have to censor him.
He liked to call a spade a spade
And toss among the glum and staid
A poem like a hand grenade –
And I remember clearly how
(Truth is the only poet's vow)
When my spare tyre was half this size,
With drumming veins and bloodshot eyes
I blundered through the rain and sleet
To dip my wick in Castle Street,
Not on the footpath – no, in a flat,
With a sofa where I often sat,
Smoked, drank, cursed, in the company
Of a female student who unwisely
Did not mind but would pull the curtain
Over the window – And did a certain
Act occur? It did. It did.
As Byron wrote of Sennacherib –
'The Assyrian came down like a wolf on the fold
And his cohorts were gleaming in purple and gold' –
But now, at nearly forty-two,
An inmate of the social zoo,
Married, baptized, well heeled, well shod,
Almost on speaking terms with God,
I intend to save my moral bacon

By fencing the young from fornication!
Ah, Dr Williams, I agree
We need more walls at the Varsity;
The students who go double-flatting
With their she-catting and tom-catting
Won't ever get a pass in Latin;
The moral mainstay of the nation
Is careful, private masturbation;
A vaseline jar or a candle
Will drive away the stink of scandal!
The Golden Age will come again –
Those tall asthenic bird-like men
With spectacles and lecture notes,
Those girls with wool around their throats
Studying till their eyes are yellow
A new corrupt text of *Othello*,
Vaguely agnostic, rationalist,
A green banana in each fist
To signify the purity
Of educational ecstasy –
And, if they marry, they will live
By the Clinical Imperative:
A car, a fridge, a radiogram,
A clean well-fitted diaphragm,
Two-and-a-half children per
Family; to keep out thunder
Insurance policies for each;
A sad glad fortnight at the beach
Each year, when Mum and Dad will bitch
From some old half-forgotten itch –
Turn on the lights! – or else the gas!
If I kneel down like a stone at Mass
And wake my good wife with bad dreams,
And scribble verse on sordid themes,
At least I know man was not made
On the style of a slot-machine arcade –
Almost, it seems, the other day,
When Francis threw his coat away
And stood under the palace light

Naked in the Bishop's sight
To marry Lady Poverty
In folly and virginity,
The angels laughed – do they then weep
Tears of blood if two should sleep
Together and keep the cradle warm?
Each night of earth, though the wind storm,
Black land behind, white sea in front,
Leander swims the Hellespont;
To Hero's bed he enters cold;
And he will drown; and she grow old –
But what they tell each other there
You'll not find in a book anywhere.

1967 1967

Tangi

to my wife

You had tied green leaves around your head;
I laced a green branch in my lapel.
On the concrete path to the meeting house
It was the women who cried out,

Calling and replying, the voice of those
Who have accepted death. And inside the door
(A thing unacceptable to the world we inhabit, in which
No one is allowed to speak of death)

The dead man was conqueror!
I saw him lying in the open boat
Of his own coffin, with shut eyes, winged moustache;
Though his widow was weeping, he was not,

And I knew for the first time the meaning of
The yellow woven tukutuku panels,
The shark's tooth, the flounder, the tears of the albatross,
Understandable only when death is accepted

As the centre of life – The opening of a million doors!
The rush of canoes that carry through breaking waves
The dead and the living! – I was glad to be
Participant. I washed my hands before eating.

1967 1969

The Rock Woman

Here the south sea washes
Kelpbed and margin of the drumhard sand.
Its grey surf-pillars thundering
Concede no altar, no denial
But an obscure torment
At the mind's edge trembling, about to be.

Continually, as a boy, I came to this
Rock ledge above the sinuous wave
Where dogs and gulls left excrement,
As if the sea-split ground could set at ease
The wish to be no longer man
That wrenched me then, that overstrides me now.

A rock carved like a woman,
Pain's torso, guardian of the place,
Told raining beads. I did not know
What grief her look wrung dry,
In what blind rooms and tombs
I and my fellows would walk heavily.

Magdalen of the rock
Unvirgin pray for us.
In the wave's throb our agonies awake
Rise to your true-all-suffering kiss.
In hewn rock of prayer
You ask for us the death hour's peace.

1955–68 *1969*

The Fear of Change

If you and I were woken suddenly
By the drums of Revolution in the street –
Or suppose the door shot open, and there stood
Upright and singing a young bullfighter

With a skin of rough wine, offering to each of us
Death, sex, hope – or even just an
Earthquake, making the trees thrash, the roofs tumble,
Calling us loudly to consider God –

Let us admit, with no shame whatever,
We are not that kind of people;
We have learnt to weigh each word like an ounce of butter;
Our talent is for anger and monotony –

Therefore we will survive the singers,
The fighters, the so-called lovers – we will bury them
Regretfully, and spend a whole wet Sunday
Arguing whether the corpses were dressed in black or red.

1967 *1976*

Spring

Girls like red-hot peonies (how nakedly they dress!);
Invisible fingers tugging at my fly;
The sense of being in a bent glass funnel –
Is it the devil? No;

It is the Lord's female lieutenant,
Venus, for once without her brother Death,
Who makes the hard twigs burst – who makes me notice
My own woman's dark mane of hair.

1967 *1976*

Summer 1967

Summer brings out the girls in their green dresses
Whom the foolish might compare to daffodils,
Not seeing how a dead grandmother in each one governs her limbs,
Darkening the bright corolla, using her lips to speak through,
Or that a silver torque was woven out of
The roots of wet speargrass.
                              The young are mastered by the Dead,
Lacking cunning. But on the beaches, under the clean wind
That blows this way from the mountains of Peru,
Drunk with the wind and the silence, not moving an inch
As the surf-swimmers mount on yoked waves,
One can begin to shake with laughter,
Becoming oneself a metal Neptune.
                              To want nothing is
The only possible freedom. But I prefer to think of
An afternoon spent drinking rum and cloves
In a little bar, just after the rain had started, in another time
Before we began to die – the taste of boredom on the tongue
Easily dissolving, and the lights coming on –
With what company? I forget.

Where can we find the right
Herbs, drinks, bandages to cover
These lifelong intolerable wounds?
Herbs of oblivion, they lost their power to help us
The day that Aphrodite touched her mouth to ours.

1967 *1973*

The Caryatids

Between night and morning but belonging to neither,
The hour when stars lean down to the earth with black flames
That the wise might use as a time for praying or writing letters;
We are not wise.
                    In a bedroom with a steel basin
And a suitcase, being insomniac,
One of us will finally beckon out of the wall
The mad boathouse-keeper with his box of photographs
Whom poets have called Eros.
                              Thinking about women –
And lighting one cigarette from another, while the white globe
Burns as it were on the roof of a cabin in a ship that carries us
                                        towards death
With no Brendan's isle to visit – we are driven to acknowledge
The ones that we loved best were the ones who broke us
Limb by limb – those natures uncorrupted by compassion
Except for a sparrow or a cat – they handled words like ploughshares –
As one lifted her face from a stunted field of rocks and grass,
Shouting – 'I will not!' – to her God; not to any man –
And one round-faced girl offered herself to be kissed, then wiped
                                        her mouth and said –
'You are – *nothing!*' And one, a drunk voice on the telephone,
                                        muttering –
'The man I love has two phalluses!'
These are the deaf caryatids,
These and their companions, each with the same limbs
And a different soul, who taught us that the flesh is human

And superhuman, lifting up on bruised shoulders
Ton by ton, the pediment of night and day.

1967 *1976*

The Doctrine

It was hope taught us to tell these lies on paper.
Scratch a poet and you will find
A small boy looking at his own face in water
Or an adolescent gripping imaginary lovers.
And the hope became real, not in action but in words,
Since words are more than nine-tenths of life.
We did not believe ourselves. Others believed us
Because they could not bear to live without some looking-glass.

'Are they real?' you ask — 'Did these things happen?'
My friend, I think of the soul as an amputee,
Sitting in a wheel-chair, perhaps in a sun-room
Reading letters, or in front of an open coal-range
Remembering a shearing gang — the bouts, the fights —
What we remember is never the truth;
And as for the body, what did it ever give us
But pain and limit? Freedom belongs to the mind.

That boy who went out and gazed at his face in the river
Was changed, they say, into a marvellous flower
Perpetually renewed in each Greek summer
Long after his tough companions had become old bones.
To act is to die. We ward off our death
With a murmuring of words.

1967 *1976*

Here

Here where the creek runs out between two rocks
And the surf can be heard a mile inland,
And the toi-tois hide the nests of a hundred birds,
And the logs lie in the swamp like the bones of giants,
And weed is rotting in heaps on the surface of the lagoon,
And the cliff shuts out the sun even at midday,
And the track peters out in banks of seagrass –

Here, where only the wind moves,
I and my crooked shadow
Bring with us briefly the colour of identity and death.

1967 *1973*

The Black Star

I do not know when exactly we saw the black star rise
Above the mountains and fields and the places where we
Were accustomed to gather. The colour of the earth was changed
As if by mildew. It was a calm day,
If I remember rightly, with a dry wind blowing over
The fruit-bearing plateau. Blossoms were falling that day
Onto our heads, into the wine
We had set out on tables. Then a child shouted,
'Look at the black star!'
                We looked up and saw it,
A spot, a disc, a kind of hole through which
The blue water of the sky was being drained out;
Yet the sun was still there, the wind kept blowing,
The wine held its savour.
                  There were a few among us
Who wept, pierced themselves with thorns, and cried,
'Deliver us, Christ, from our sin!'
                What sin?

Sins are bred in the marrow of the bones of men,
Painful no doubt, but the wisest learn to live with them.
I forgot to say some of us began to scatter paper money
On the greying earth. No one would stoop to pick it up.
The old people now keep close to their houses,
And the young have grown ungovernable – they run wild
                                                    wearing masks
Of hair and stick and bone. The middle-aged are finding it
Tolerable; at least I do.
                  As for the black star,
It whirls, it stands, it governs the day and the night,
And though we prefer not to speak about it,
We regard it in a sense as a new god – god or machine – we call it
The Equalizer.

1968 *1976*

The Bargain

The rows of pea-plants in my neighbour's garden
Glisten with the dew. Paths of wet asphalt

Climb the near-by hill, under some kind of tree
Whose leaves topple in green waterfalls,

Leading very likely to a car-park or a junk-yard
But able to be thought of as the wandering track

That goes to a place where Brother Ass can bray
Without burdens. I can smoke, type letters, wind

The cuckoo clock, drink lukewarm coffee
In my scrubbed house – I have accepted God's bribe,

To be content with not being dead,
His singing eunuch – and my son who clatters

His hippie bells from room to room, my wife
Who makes pies out of buttered bread at the white range,

Even the grey cat blinking and curling its claws
In the armchair, are certain the bargain's a right one –

Yet if the prisoner ceased one day to sweat and rage
In his cell of jumping nerves and layered muscle,

Dreaming of wild women and guerilla battles,
Bridges blown up, farewells in African hovels,

I would not be I, and the bargain useless,
For He would be cheated of the aroma of bitter blood

Spilt on the cross-tree, and I would have become
Simply the dead man hanging, the abdicated Jesus.

1968 1974

Stephanie

Stepping so early out of the womb of heaven
Down to a cluttered room with a Ravi Shankar
Record playing – and, I must add, your grandfather Sisyphus
(Myself) smoking a hundred brown
Cigarettes – I acknowledge, my only and therefore favourite
Grandchild, you have betrayed me into
Uncalled-for tremors of joy in the rock of the heart
It is my business to shove uphill each day –
O what if it should split!
                    The epicanthic fold
You inherit from your grandmother's people and share
Equally with the ghost of Te Rauparaha
And those who have dammed the waters of the Yang Tse,
Our neighbours over the wall – that tightly drawn
Arrested fold of skin which frames the dark-blue eye

You fix me with, as I feed you from a bottle heated
In the electric jug, provides what I cannot name
Except as arrows of religious hope
Transfixing an atheist.
                              To believe in love
Is difficult. It means that we cannot belong
Any more to ourselves, having suffered a foreign invasion
From heaven. Stephanie, I confess with terrified
Acquiescence, your springtime banners are inside my gate.

                              October 1968, Hocken MS 975/16

To Patric Carey

From beaches grey with ambergris
The pressure of invention came,
Like waves that penetrate through combs of sand,
That single, first, unknowable proposition
Published in theatres of stone
By actors roaring through great hollow masks
Not thunder, no, but the life of Aeschylus
Decaying to a hard wave-polished bone.

And still the mouths of actors vend
With Beckett, Brecht and Behan, what
The audiences know as well
As blood and semen, but forget,
That we are gaps in banks of broken sand:
Lucky the playwright then who keeps
After the public stoning and the praise,
Silence and one producer as a friend.

                              23 December 1968 *1979*

Letter to Sam Hunt

Dear Sam, I thank you for your letter
And for the poem too, much better
To look at than the dreary words
I day by day excrete like turds
To help the Catholic bourgeoisie
To bear their own insanity;
And if in Paremata you
Should find a weta in your shoe,
Ugly, hard-shelled, with snapping jaws,
A Hitler who has lost his cause,
Don't hit it with a shovel – No,
Christen it JIM and let it go.

Though it may serve no good, in rhyme,
To look back on the fucking-time,
I do recall one evening, drunk
In Devonport on Dally plonk,
Endangering my balls and marriage
With someone's darling in a garage,
Upright and groaning, breaking eggs
Until the yolk ran down her legs –
One of the best of Venus' nuns,
A girl with tits like ack–ack guns
Who sighed and screwed and screwed and sighed
While her grim husband sat inside
The house and meditated death
For her and me with every breath,
Journalist, tombstone-maker, or
Some other kind of social whore.
Last year we met again and she
Not screwing sighed and looked at me,
A swaddled deathshead old and dry,
But there was life in that blue eye.

'Honey,' I said, 'You're thinking of
Another time when love was love.'

'You've struck it, brother,' she replied,
'But now I find the gap inside
Is cold and dark and hard to carry
And Buddha is the man I marry;
He teaches me that love is love
Only when it's past thinking of.'

Dear Sam, if you are twenty-two,
Why should I foist my gall on you?
The answer is that poets live
By a refusal to forgive
The mighty Bog of social shit
That has no use for sex or wit
Or art or hope, but simply is
Internally its own abyss;
At twenty-two or forty-one
You need your gumboots and a gun.

Sam Hunt, Sam Hunt, Sam Hunt, Sam Hunt,
The housewife with her oyster cunt
Has pissed upon what might have been
Lively, original and green,
The old pohutukawa tree
With hairy ballocks on its knee.
The Pill, the Rags, the Summer Sale,
Put Venus and her tribes in jail
Till every fuck's a coffin-nail;
Her husband, that sad pudding-head,
Will pull himself each night in bed
Softly, for fear he'll wake the Dead,
And teach his children how to lick
The Boss's arse and not be sick, –
Not that I blame the poor blind bitch
Who hoped that she would strike it rich
But saw her pretty flowers wilt,
Her cunt turn into a patchwork quilt,
Her handsome Prince become a Frog,
And drowned herself in the Social Bog.

But I must go my own way still
Across Death Brig and up Skull Hill
To learn the science of our grief
Conversing with the Impenitent Thief,
The one unique left-handed saint
Who knows why we must write and paint.
He teaches me that Sophocles
Heard in the thunder of Greek seas
On beaches grey with ambergris,
On the recoiling serpent hiss
A voice proclaiming to the land
That men are banks of broken sand,
And various other things that I
May put in plays before I die.

Dear Sam, this day as I came down
The steps that take me into town,
Rehearsing in my head these rhymes
That hold a mirror to the times,
A perfect omen crossed my track,
A garbage-eater, wild and black,
Pugnacious, paranoid and sly,
A tomcat with a boxer's eye
Dripping a gum of yellow pus,
I thought that he resembled us
Who may write poems well, with luck,
About the dolls we do not fuck,
And hear the dark creek water flow
From a rock gate we do not know.
Till we ourselves become that breach
And silence is our only speech.

1968 *1973*

THE JERUSALEM PERIOD

Ans Westra

By the beginning of 1970 Baxter's Jerusalem commune was well underway. His intention was to form a community structured around key 'spiritual aspects of Maori communal life', to recover values New Zealand's Pākehā urban society had lost. He first recorded aspects of his philosophy of communality in *Jerusalem Sonnets: Poems for Colin Durning* (1970). The thirty-nine sonnets – which may as readily be understood as a long poem in thirty-nine stanzas – were sent, during the first phase of the Jerusalem commune, with letters written to Durning, Baxter's friend and confidant. Appropriately, they form an extended verse epistle, their loose, unrhymed couplets (reflecting Lawrence Durrell's influence) expressing friendship, discussing everyday life, and meditating on God. There are hints of a restless quest for meaning in references to journeys, but Baxter also reflects on the ubiquitous 'gap': that place of stillness, where the mind is silenced and God is experienced. Behind their deceptive simplicity the poems display a remarkable unity of voice, theme and setting. With humour and piety, in tones both personal and universal, Baxter's sonnets create that 'tension of belief' that, he once stated, 'gives the poem its edge'.

Jerusalem Daybook (1971) is the first of Baxter's volumes to combine verse with prose. It expresses Baxter's personal perspective on the practice and philosophy of communalism as it relates to the initial phase of his Jerusalem commune. In practice, the commune lacked order: Baxter could not regulate numbers or behaviour, the media sensationalised his activities, and the locals became increasingly uneasy. Problems were compounded because he was often away – in Dunedin visiting his dying father; on speaking tours; and on 8 February 1971 protesting with young Māori radicals at Waitangi.

The commune's first phase ended in September 1971 and Baxter returned to Wellington, where he lived for a time in squats and wrote some of his most scathing poetry. But in February 1972 the Jerusalem land-owners permitted him to return with a smaller, more cohesive, group. His last collection, *Autumn Testament* (1972), dates from this period. Published shortly after his death in 1972, it comprises three poetic and two prose sequences. Two short poems bracket the titlepiece. The first of these, 'He Waiata mo Te Kare', is Baxter's final verse letter to his wife; the second, 'Te Whiore o te Kuri' – 'the tail of the dog / That wags at the end of my book' – is a sequence of seven sonnets. The forty-eight sonnets of the title poem document the life of the Jerusalem community and appear to anticipate Baxter's own end. But his characteristic imagery of death, often a disturbing feature of his poetry, now suggests peace and acceptance.

At around the same time as Baxter was seeing *Autumn Testament* through to publication, he was working on another selection, *Runes*, for Oxford University Press. He may have written, in 1968, 'The book is shut and I have gone / In rags to serve the Virgin's Son', but Baxter continued to value his earlier writing. *Runes* is therefore a testament of a different sort: in its broad selection from the poetry of the preceding two decades there lies a statement about the value of art.

By August 1972 Baxter was drained, physically and emotionally. He sought refuge on a small commune in Auckland. On 22 October he died of a coronary thrombosis.

A memorable literary and spiritual commemoration ensued. His body was escorted back by his family to Jerusalem where, in a rare honour for a Pākehā, he received a full Māori tangi and was buried on tribal land, attended by hundreds of people from the many walks of life with which Baxter's intersected. A boulder inscribed 'HEMI / JAMES KEIR BAXTER / I WHANAU 1926 / I MATE 1972' marks the grave.

[The book is shut]

The book is shut and I have gone
In rags to serve the Virgin's Son
James K. Baxter he is dead;
Plant a boulder at his head
And write on it – 'Goodbye, good luck,
The words are somewhere in the book;
This bloke inside a broken heart
Carried the spike of time and art,
But now he does another thing
With silence for a wedding ring –
Christ and Mary, greet your guest;
Memine, nihil satis est. Amen.'

1968 *2001*

For Hone

Tuakana, I am a hard stone
Thrown from a heavy sling

Breaking through walls and padlocked doors
That time has rusted fast

'Ko wai koe? Ko wai koe?
Te tangi o te manu.'

Tuakana, now I wear your coat
I am a stone man walking

And in the cold night of the town
The gravestones are all shaped like women.

The coat will keep me warm when I lie down.
The cigarette burn on the left side of it

Is better than a pocket full of money.

13 March 1969 *1979*

from *Ballad of the Junkies and the Fuzz*

for Hoani

1

Oh star I do not believe in, speak to me!
Star of the harbour night, wave after wave rising and falling
Under the bows of the Devonport ferry that carries a cargo of
                              people home to their well-lit prisons,
Boys half lushed and girls in jeans or party dresses, older men
                      looking vacantly at the black waves, women
                          who do not show their souls in their eyes —
Star I do not believe in, shining also
In the rickety streets of Grafton where many gather
In a single house, sharing the kai, sharing the pain, sharing the
                              drug perhaps, sharing the paranoia;
Bearded, barefoot or sandalled, coming out crippled from the bin
                                                  or the clink.
(The windows painted black; yet the black paint was scraped off
                                                  again) —
In order that the junkie rock may crack and flow with water
And the rainbow of aroha shine on each one's face
Because love is in the look, stronger than lush, and truth is in the
                              mouth, better than kai —
Rain down your light, oh star of paradise!

3

Baron Saturday, baron of the cemeteries, for whom they cut the
                      black rooster's throat, whose altar is
                          always a grave at the crossroads,
You have shifted, man, out of thin Haiti. Now you grow fat on the
                  fears of five thousand junkies in Auckland.

How strange, man, to see those spruce and angry ghosts
Suddenly materialize
In an old house in the middle of the morning
When several are eating soup, one is playing the guitar, two are
                                  talking about nasturtium leaves,
And the others are snoring after an all-night party –
Suddenly you see them in the centre of the room,
The servants of the Zombie King –
Skorbul the football player with his brown moustache,
Krubble, who has a habit of crushing fingers in doors,
Drooble, who is glad to bang girls' heads on walls,
And one or two other clean-cut eager beagles
Young poltergeists squaring their shoulders, imitating the TV
                                  hero, hoping for a punch-up –
The fuzz are in the house.

'Would you like a coffee, Mr Skorbul?'
'Naow.'
'A cup of soup then?'
'Naow. What y' bin doing round here?'

Star I do not believe in, let your tendrils of light grow
And out of them it may be we can make a vine ladder
To climb back to where God is, that high blue room in the sky.

4

On the wall at the bottom of my bed somebody has painted
A girl with a helmet of blue and white jungle flowers,
And the white centre of the largest bloom
Is the centre of the brain – I think she must be well stoned
On coke or morph, this heavy-lidded Lilith
Who was the first wife, the one whom Adam created
Out of a solitary imagination
When the world was very young – I do not mind at all
Having her watch me while I sleep.

5

It was necessary of course to invent the fuzz
To fence off the area of civilized coma
From the forces of revolt and lamentation
That rise around it, male and female
Ikons weeping tears of blood.

1969 *1970*

Jerusalem Sonnets
Poems for Colin Durning

*If that Jerusalem which is unshakeable
friendship with God has not first been
established in the heart, how can the
objective Jerusalem of communal charity
be built so as not to fall?*

1

The small grey cloudy louse that nests in my beard
Is not, as some have called it, 'a pearl of God' –

No, it is a fiery tormentor
Waking me at two a.m.

Or thereabouts, when the lights are still on
In the houses in the pa, to go across thick grass

Wet with rain, feet cold, to kneel
For an hour or two in front of the red flickering

Tabernacle light – what He sees inside
My meandering mind I can only guess –

A madman, a nobody, a raconteur
Whom He can joke with – 'Lord,' I ask Him,

'Do You or don't You expect me to put up with lice?'
His silent laugh still shakes the hills at dawn.

2

The bees that have been hiving above the church porch
Are some of them killed by the rain –

I see their dark bodies on the step
As I go in – but later on I hear

Plenty of them singing with what seems a virile joy
In the apple tree whose reddish blossoms fall

At the centre of the paddock – there's an old springcart,
Or at least two wheels and the shafts, upended

Below the tree – Elijah's chariot it could be, Colin,
Because my mind takes fire a little there

Thinking of the woman who is like a tree
Whom I need not name – clumsily gripping my beads,

While the bees drum overhead and the bouncing calves look at
A leather-jacketed madman set on fire by the wind.

3

A square picture of that old man of Ars
Whom the devil so rightly cursed as a potato-eater

Hangs on the wall not far from the foot of my bed –
Gently he smiles at me when I undo my belt

And begin to hit my back with the two brass rings
On the end of it – twenty strokes are more than enough –

Soon I climb wincing into my sleeping bag
And say to him – 'Old man, how can I,

'Smoking, eating grapefruit, hack down the wall of God?'
'By love,' he answers, 'by love, my dear one,

'By love alone' – and his hippie hairdo flutters
In a wind from beyond the stars, while I stretch out and dream

Of going with Yvette in a shaky aeroplane
Across a wide black gale-thrashed sea.

4

The high green hill I call Mount Calvary
Is only perhaps a hundred feet high

But it fills the kitchen window – man, today I puffed
Up the sheeptrack ridges and found three posts at the top

Conveniently disposed – behind that a grove of pines
With trunks like – well, I thought of rafters, roof trees

And ocean-going canoes, nor did I pick up one
Cone or stick, thinking – 'They belong to Te Tama

'In whose breast the world is asleep' – but when I came
Back down the gully a wild calf with a

Tubular protruding eye, white
Around its edges, jerking in the socket,

Ran from me – wisely, wisely,
Smelling the master of all who is never himself.

5

Man, my outdoor lavatory
Has taken me three days to build –

A trench cut deep into the clay,
Then four posts, some rusty fencing wire

And a great fort of bracken
Intertwined – a noble structure

Like the gardens of Babylon, made to hide
My defecation from the eyes of the nuns –

And this morning I found a fat green frog
Squatting in the trench – I lifted him out

Against his will and set him free,
But I am trapped in the ditch of ownership

Wondering if the next gale at night
Will flatten the whole ziggurat and leave me to shit naked.

6

The moon is a glittering disc above the poplars
And one cloud travelling low down

Moves above the house – but the empty house beyond,
Above me, over the hill's edge,

Knotted in bramble is what I fear,
Te whare kehua – love drives, yet I draw back

From going step by step in solitude
To the middle of the Maori night

Where dreams gather – those hard steps taken one by one
Lead out of all protection, and even a crucifix

Held in the palm of the hand will not fend off
Precisely that hour when the moon is a spirit

And the wounds of the soul open – to be is to die
The death of others, having loosened the safe coat of becoming.

7

My visitors have now departed,
Jill and Maori Johnny – they taught me to swear again

And brought me bad news of Boyle Crescent,
The junkies pigeon-roost,

House of sorrow, house of love
To which my riderless soul night after night returns,

Neighing – 'Where are you?' It seems that somebody lit
A fire in the cellar, and two rooms were burnt out –

The wise tribe have left – Gipsy, Norma,
Yancy, Robert – the bones of my arms are aching

To hold them, my eyes want to look
On the streets of Grafton, where I was a king

For a little while – but the house of wood and straw
Is gone in smoke, and I am branded by that fire.

8

Many may think it out of date
That I should bend my back in a field,

Eat watercress, catch lice and pray –
'Moderation suits our time; moreover

'An educated rational approach
May set the young folk a good example

'In their adjustment' – any priest in town could tell me that;
I do not go by the priests; I go by what

My thirteen-year-old son Hoani told me
Before he left the Buddha to use a hypodermic –

'Live sparely; laugh at money;
Follow uphill the track of the bull –

'Can a snowflake exist in a raging fire?
Here are the footprints of the patriarchs.'

9

The crabs have returned – no creatures more communal,
Determined to be at one with their sad host,

They hang their egg-bags just above ground level
At the roots of hairs – or that is what I think

After investigation – perhaps bi-sexual,
With the double force of a mother's and a father's

Love they dig in like the troops in shellholes
Of World War One – so numerous a nation,

There's no danger, man, of genocide
Though I afflict them with pure Dettol

Time and again – I'd like to sign a truce –
'Have my moustache; and leave the rest free!'

But they have no Pope or King, Colin;
Anarchist, acephalous; they've got me stuffed!

10

Dark night – or rather, only the stars
Somebody called 'those watchfires in the sky' –

Too cold for me the thoughts of God – I crossed
The paddock on another errand,

And the cows were slow to move outside the gate
Where they sleep at night – nevertheless I came

As it were by accident into the church
And knelt again in front of the tabernacle,

His fortress – man, His thoughts are not cold!
I dare not say what fire burned then, burns now

Under my breastbone – but He came back with me
To my own house, and let this madman eat,

And shared my stupid prayer, and carried me up
As the mother eagle lifts her fluttering young with her wings.

11

One writes telling me I am her guiding light
And my poems her bible – on this cold morning

After mass I smoke one cigarette
And hear a magpie chatter in the paddock,

The image of Hatana – he bashes at the windows
In idiot spite, shouting – 'Pakeha! You can be

'The country's leading poet' – at the church I murmured, 'Tena koe'
To the oldest woman and she replied, 'Tena koe' –

Yet the red book is shut from which I should learn Maori
And these daft English words meander on,

How dark a light! Hatana, you have gripped me
Again by the balls; you sift and riddle my mind

On the rack of the middle world, and from my grave at length
A muddy spring of poems will gush out.

12

'Mother Mary Joseph Aubert, did you come here
To civilize the Maoris?' – 'No, my son,

'I came from my native France to these rough hills
Only to make them Christian' – 'Why then, mother,

'Are the corners of your mouth drawn down,
Why do you frown a little, why are your old hands folded

'In a rheumatic clench?' – 'Work, work;
Without work nobody gets to Heaven' –

'There's no work for the Maori in the towns' –
'Nonsense! There is always work, if one can

'Be tidy, chaste, well spoken' – 'The pa is all but empty,
Old woman, where you fought your fight

'And planted cherry trees – Pray for the converts' great-grandchildren
Who need drugs to sleep at night.'

13

It is not possible to sleep
As I did once in Grafton

Under the bright candles of a poor man's wall,
Under the delicate Japanese image

Of the Man dying whose arms embrace the night –
Lying curled in rough blankets, perhaps alone,

Perhaps not alone, with the great freedom
Of a river that runs in the dark towards its mouth –

Oh treasure of the poor, to be loved!
Arms and eyes I shall not see again –

It is not possible to sleep
The sleep of children, sweeter than marihuana,

Or to be loved so dearly as we have been loved,
With our weapons thrown down, for a breathing space.

14

I had lain down for sleep, man, when He called me
To go across the wet paddock

And burgle the dark church – you see, Colin, the nuns
Bolt the side door and I unbolt it

Like a timid thief – red light, moonlight
Mix together; steps from nowhere

Thud in the porch; a bee wakes up and buzzes;
The whole empty pa and the Maori dead

Are present – there I lie down cruciform
On the cold linoleum, a violator

Of God's decorum – and what has He to tell me?
'More stupid than a stone, what do you know

'Of love? Can you carry the weight of my Passion,
You old crab farmer?' I go back home in peace.

15

To give away cigarettes,
That's the hard one, Colin!

To live on rolled oats, raisins,
Potatoes, milk, raw cabbage,

It's even a pleasure – but I confess I need a smoke
More than I need a woman!

It's more like breathing – ever since I broached the guests' tobacco
(Along with the guests) I've been a doomed man!

Perhaps earlier yet – at six years old,
When I kept what I stole from my father in a rusty tin

Under the house, mixed with old rotted
Cabbage tree fibres – was it original virtue

Or original sin? I roll it now, and draw deep
The herb of darkness, preferring Nirvana to Heaven.

16

'Suburban street like sea of glass' –
'Plan to deafen Loch Ness monster' –

'Mayor denies link with Mafia gangsters' –
'Control that's light, fantastic, lovely,

'Under shorts or skirts' – the deaf blind world
Howling on all fours would like to deafen

Its imaginary brother, the great water lizard?
Can the Hell's Angels get to Heaven

Striding over broken teeth and glass?
Did you have your bra on, lady, when they took you to the bin?

Who is the gangster? I am only half sane
But the sane half tells me that newspapers were made

For wiping arses and covering tables,
Not for reading – now, man, I have a table cloth.

17

I went up barefoot to te whare kehua
This morning – but it seemed the earthquake god

Had been before me, represented by
Two young Maoris with a cunning bulldozer

That ripped up posts, earth, bramble, everything standing,
And left – well, the house

With its broken window, ghosts and lumber,
Severely out of date – I went in, treading

Carefully, to avoid a rotted kit, and knelt down
In front of the picture somebody had left to guard

The place – a cloudgazing pakeha Christ
With His heart in His hand, well felted against the weather –

And I said – 'Brother, when will your Maori church be built?
When will you hoist us all out of the graveyard?'

18

Yesterday I planted garlic,
Today, sunflowers – 'the non-essentials first'

Is a good motto – but these I planted in honour of
The Archangel Michael and my earthly friend,

Illingworth, Michael also, who gave me the seeds –
And they will turn their wild pure golden discs

Outside my bedroom, following Te Ra
Who carries fire for us in His terrible wings

(Heresy, man!) – and if He wanted only
For me to live and die in this old cottage,

It would be enough, for the angels who keep
The very stars in place resemble most

These green brides of the sun, hopelessly in love with
Their Master and Maker, drunkards of the sky.

19

At the centre of my mind the stone lies
And the bullock bleeds there – be it so,

Be it so, be it so,
Now and – you know, Colin,

What I mean when I say, 'Te Kare' – my life winds out
And winds back to that hard stone,

The rock of unknowing – this old bullock will kick
Once or twice, but offers himself again

To the knife of love – Te Kare, wave of the sea
On which the Dove moved before the world began,

For you I weep, for you I become a child,
Since only children have power to grip the lightning

Unharmed – by doing nothing I will do
What you desire, and bring you one day to the earthly garden.

20

The ring I wear on my third finger
(Alan Thornton gave me it) – one fish

For te ihi, the force of life in man;
Two fishes for Te Kare and myself,

The love of the One to the One which is the hook in our guts;
Three fishes for the Many, the cross of Te Ariki

That breaks out in flower; the anchor, te aroha –
I have worn it now, Colin, for eight months

Or thereabouts – it burns me and it saves me –
Or say the single one is the pakeha fish

And the big one Te Ariki
Followed by te tuna, the Maori fish

Who twists on after Him in poverty and darkness,
And I must go with them upstream to the heart of the cross.

21

Can this poor donkey ever carry Him
Into Hiruharama? Everything stands against it,

But that is the Rider's problem – on my kitchen shelf I keep
The square awkward tin that Agnes gave me

The day I left here going north,
A blind man walking – inside she put for me

Bread and cake and potted eel
To give me strength on that slow journey

To the mills of Hatana – now I am back here again;
The bread is gone, the eel is eaten,

And Hatana has written on the marrow of my bones
One kind of understanding – Agnes, I think, is out of it –

In Wanganui in her sister's house
Where the trees are cut down by the chainsaw and the ripsaw.

22

Let the Maker of rainbows and mountains do what He wishes
With this poor idiot, this crab in His beard

Who will not be dislodged – becoming, as it were,
Available is all my science,

And what He will do He will do – the problem is
Not our existence, Colin, but our arrogance

That wants to run the party – tomorrow I plant potatoes
With any luck, secretly nourishing them

With my own dung, carried with a trowel
From the giant maimai – not wishing to scandalize

Anybody – that is one job I can do
While He lets me do it; another is to pray

That He'll send me, in His good time, a tuakana
To work alongside me and instruct me in these matters.

23

First I strip the sods off; then I shake them
To get the earth loose, and carry them

A few yards to make a wall that might
Shelter some beans – Sister Aquinas in her

Dark blue dress hoeing beside the cowshed
Tells me – 'The couch grass seems to grow the more,

'The more you cultivate' – I lay the long white roots
Inside a broken tank for the sun to kill

By slow roasting; and begin to spade the earth,
Diagonally of course – this man has to make a game

Even out of digging; my pants and shirt
From Father Te Awhitu; my boots from the Vincent de Paul

Society – when the wind flutters round my chest
It seems to say, 'Now, now, don't be proud that you are poor!'

24

The kids here don't shout out, 'Jesus!'
Or, 'Hullo, Moses!' as they did in Auckland

When they saw my hair – these ones are too polite –
They call me Mr Baxter when they bring the milk;

I almost wish they didn't; but Sister has them well trained –
And soon she wants me to give them a talk about drugs;

What should I say? – 'Children, your mothers and your fathers
Get stoned on grog; in Auckland they get stoned on pot;

'It does no harm at all, as far as I know
From smoking it; but the big firms are unloading

'Pep pills for slimming, tablets for sleeping,
On the unlucky world – those ones can drive you mad –

'Money and prestige are worse drugs than morphine' –
That way I'd hit the target; but I doubt if the nuns would think it
wise.

25

The brown river, te taniwha, flows on
Between his banks – he could even be on my side,

I suspect, if there is a side – there are still notches worn
In the cliffs downstream where they used to shove

The big canoes up; and just last week some men
Floated a ridge-pole down from an old pa

For the museum – he can also be
A brutal lover; they say he sucked under

A young girl once, and the place at the river-bend is named
After her tears – I accept that – I wait for

The taniwha in the heart to rise – when will that happen?
Is He dead or alive? A car goes by on the road

With an enormous slogan advertising
Rides for tourists on the jetboat at Pipiriki.

26

'Under a naked Master it does not fit well
The disciple to be too dainty' – so I paraphrase

The words of Bernard; for comfort, Colin, comfort
May kill the heart – so then, if the Dettol burns my jowls,

If the earth splits my fingers, if the wind is sharp
Blowing from banks of cloud as I go out

In a thin shirt, it is only to avoid
Being too dainty – the yogi Milarepa,

My son told me, lived for years on nettle soup
And his sister called him a fool – 'an ascetic hedonist',

Our theologians might comment – but how do they fight
The world and the flesh in their universities?

The naked Master who hangs above my door
Gave up, like old Milarepa, His bones to the bonfire.

27

Three dark buds for the Trinity
On one twig I found in the lining of my coat

Forgotten since I broke them from the tree
That grows opposite the RSA building

At the top of Vulcan Lane – there I would lay down my parka
On the grass and meditate, cross-legged; there was a girl

Who sat beside me there;
She would hold a blue flower at the centre of the bullring

While the twigs on the tree became black
And then slowly green again – she was young – if I had said,

'Have my coat; have my money' –
She would have gone away; but because I gave her nothing

She came again and again to share that nothing
Like a bird that nests in the open hand.

28

In a room full of smoke now that the stove is lit
The feeling of being on a space-ship bound for Mars

Is taking charge – the wing of the noonday demon,
I think, though he happens to visit me at night,

The hermit's familiar – What does he say? – something
Like this – 'You should be somewhere else, brother,

'Anywhere else; this stagnant life is bad,
Much too limited for a bloke of your talents

'Such as – well, you name them! – in the frame of modern life
You'd be better off doing – it doesn't matter what,

'As long as it isn't – well, digging in cow manure,
Eating, sleeping' – (he doesn't mention praying) –

'And as for that notion of yours of founding a tribe,
Hell, you're on your own here!' – I squash him like a weta with
                                              the shovel.

29

Our Lady shifted the demons; no need to talk about it;
It is her habit, lucid, warm,

Miraculous – but if you are consulted
One day, Colin, about my epitaph,

I suggest these words – 'He was too much troubled
By his own absurdity' – though I'd prefer – 'Hemi' –

And nothing else – today my new job
Is to disentangle the roots of the fourteen small

Green cabbage plants Sister Aquinas gave me
Wrapped in damp paper – one good use, man,

For the written word! – and put them in carefully
Where the beautiful loose earth is that crumbles to the blows

Of the grubber, and later give them a little water
When the sun cannot burn their delicate leaves.

30

If Ngati-Hiruharama turns out to be no more than
A child's dream in the night – well then,

I have a garden, a bed to lie on,
And various company – some clattering pigeons roost

At my back door, and when I meditate in the paddock
Under the apple tree two healthy dung-smeared pigs

Strike up a conversation, imagining, I think,
I am their benefactor – that should be quite enough

To keep the bowels moving and the mind thankful;
Yet when the sun rises my delusion hears him shout

Above the river fog – 'This is the hill fort
Of our God; it is called Hiruharama!

'The goat and the opossum will find a home
Among the rocks, and the river of joy will flow from it!'

31

Father Te Awhitu pays me a visit
Carrying a golf club; his words are clear enough

In spite of the stroke – 'Do you think, Father,
The sins of the flesh are mainly mortal?' – 'Yes' –

'It's hard in the towns' – 'Eh, the Maori can do all right;
There's no one poor in this country' –

'I spend a lot of time writing letters;
You can plant a seed, Father, but it grows by itself in the dark,

'And then only if God' – 'You know,
A thought came to me; you could write a play

'About the fight down on Moutoa Island;
A Brother was killed there' – the plate on the stove is slow

To heat up and Father leaves without his coffee;
The Maori angel has put me in my place.

32

Tormenting myself with a moral inventory
While I cut the sods and lay them straight

To make a wall to shelter beans,
I think of my two illegitimate children

And how they will judge me when they come of age;
Unfit, I grant it – yet what can a man do

Who is trying to make a wall to shelter beans
But cut the sods and lay them straight;

And what can a man do who is saddled with a woman
But love her whatever way he can

Till his guts drop out? 'Now you're a Lutheran,' mutters
The voice at my earhole; but I laugh,

Remembering the women used no rubber plugs or pills
Because they wanted to have my children.

33

Here in the morning there is no Vice Squad
To keep me on my toes – I'd cross myself once,

Say the Hail Holy Queen, then shamble out
To the kitchen to talk with Morgan – 'The house is filthy,

'Mr Baxter! That's not the way
To cure anybody' – 'Well, Mr Morgan,

'This is a kind of pakeha marae;
I'm only a lodger – you can see the one drug

'They've been using is alcohol' – Strubble would say nothing
But stroll round like a wound-up Spanish bull

While the kids climbed out of bed; I think he liked the place;
It felt like home to him – but here at 9 a.m.

There's just myself, the birds and Sister Aquinas
Knocking at the door with a bowl of dwarf beans.

34

I read it in the Maori primer,
'Ka timata te pupuhi o te hau' —

The wind began blowing; it blew for a century
Levelling by the musket and the law

Ten thousand meeting houses — there are two of them in the pa,
Neither one used; the mice and the spiders meet there;

And the tapu mound where the heads of chiefs were burned
Will serve perhaps one day for a golf course — yet

Their children fear te taipo,
The bush demon; on that account

They keep the lights burning all night outside their houses —
What can this pakeha fog-eater do?

Nothing; nothing! Tribe of the wind,
You can have my flesh for kai, my blood to drink.

35

The trap I am setting to catch a tribe
Is all but furnished — on Friday Father Condon

Will (if he remembers) bring from Ohakune
The crucifix my friend Milton carved

With its garments made of wood shavings
And a faceless face, Maori or pakeha either

As the light catches it; also the workman Buddha
Hoani lent me, and the Hindu image of Mara

Trix handed on so as to be wholly poor –
What else, Colin? They say it is best

To break a rotten egg in the creek
To get eels – I think I am that egg

And Te Ariki must crack me open
If the fish are to be drawn in at all.

36

Brother Ass, Brother Ass, you are full of fancies,
You want this and that – a woman, a thistle,

A poem, a coffeebreak, a white bed, no crabs;
And now you complain of the weight of the Rider

Who will set you free to gallop in the light of the sun!
Ah well, kick Him off then, and see how you go

Lame-footed in the brambles; your disconsolate bray
Is ugly in my ears – long ago, long ago,

The battle was fought and the issue decided
As to who would be King – go on, little donkey

Saddled and bridled by the Master of the world,
Be glad you can distinguish not an inch of the track,

That the stones are sharp, that your hide can itch,
That His true weight is heavy on your back.

37

Colin, you can tell my words are crippled now;
The bright coat of art He has taken away from me

And like the snail I crushed at the church door
My song is my stupidity;

The words of a homely man I cannot speak,
Home and bed He has taken away from me;

Like an old horse turned to grass I lift my head
Biting at the blossoms of the thorn tree;

Prayer of priest or nun I cannot use,
The songs of His house He has taken away from me;

As blind men meet and touch each other's faces
So He is kind to my infirmity;

As the cross is lifted and the day goes dark
Rule over myself He has taken away from me.

38

'I am dying now because I do not die' –
The song of the thief who hangs upon the tree;

'The house where I was born had seven windows
But its door is closed to me;

Whether I robbed or not I have forgotten,
My death has taken hold of me;

There was a woman once who gave me a cup of wine
And her eyes were full of mercy;

There is not even judgement any more
In the place where I have to be;

I cannot turn my head to find out
Who hangs beside me on the other tree;

Let the woman who is standing down below
Say a prayer for him and me.'

39

In Auckland it was the twelve days' garland,
Feast with friends and shouting in the streets;

Now it is the apex and the clean flint knife –
Colin, if you meet him, give my love

To Patric Carey, and if you have the time
Once or twice go out to Brighton

To visit my parents – easy to hang
Imperatives on a good friend from a distance,

But I say, 'If ' – one thing, how can the image come
At all to the centre where the mind is silent

Without being false? I had hoped for fifty sonnets,
But here are thirty-nine, my gift to you, Colin,

From Hiruharama,
From Hemi te tutua.

1969 1970

Haere Ra

Farewell to Hiruharama –
The green hills and the river fog
Cradling the convent and the Maori houses –

The peach tree at my door is broken, sister,
It carried too much fruit,
It hangs now by a bent strip of bark –

But better that way than the grey moss
Cloaking the branch like an old man's beard;
We are broken by the Love of the Many

And then we are at peace
Like the fog, like the river, like a roofless house
That lets the sun stream in because it cannot help it.

1969 *1979*

The Labyrinth

for John Weir

So many corridors, – so many lurches
On the uneven filthy floor
Daedalus made and then forgot, – 'What *right*
Have you to be here?' the demons thick as roaches
Whispering …
                Mind fixed on the Minotaur
I plugged onward like a camel that first night,
Thinking – 'Not long, brother, not long now!' –
But now so many nights have passed
The problem is to think of him at all
And not of, say, the fact that I am lost
Or the spark of light that fell upon my brow

From some high vault, – I sit down like a little girl
To play with my dolls, – sword, wallet and the god's great amulet

My father gave me.
                    In the bullfights it was easy
(Though heroic no doubt) because their eyes, their eyes held me
To the agile task. Now I am a child
Frightened by falling water, by each nerve-pricking memory
Of things ill done, – but I do not forget
One thing, the thread, the invisible silk I hold
And shall hold till I die.
                    I tell you, brother,
When I throw my arms around the Minotaur
Our silence will be pure as gold.

1970 1974

Meditation on my Father's Death

        Where my father walked and found
        the rock where Abraham took
        a knife to offer Isaac,
        a new tree catches the wind
        from the nut a bird dropped down
        in a crevice of the rock,

        and it sprouted and grows tall,
        leaning above the demon-
        hearted breakers and the worn
        elbows of seastone.
                    Angel
        of our dark searching, tell us
        why the dead blaze like the sun

        between our thoughts! My father
        has wood and earth on his face,
        yet hardly a flake of loss

blows to me from the bonfire
of his great joy; and I stand
barefoot under the gallows

of my forty-fourth year, gripped
by the rope of mercy, stoned
on the blood of God.
                    The wind
has blown the tree, swept and shaped
its arms to fit the earth's hard
jail where all limbs have to bend.

1970 *1979*

Winter Monologue

One has to die here on earth,
My beard has got the stink of the ground already,

The opossum thuds in the roof like a man dropping bricks,
My belly is content enough

With two cups of tea and two bits of cake
Wehe gave me today as I sat on her doorstep,

But the night comes like a hammer cracking on an anvil
And all nga mokai huddle in the big house,

Playing the guitar, lighting up the little stove,
Not finding fault – one has to die

In order to water the roots of the tree with blood,
Guts, nerves, brains – once I was a word-maker,

Now my bones are buried at Hiruharama,
But the bones talk, brother. They say – 'Winter burns us like
                                        black fire!'

Ah well, soon I will go up the hill
To where the drain and the ditch and the new pipe

Are tangled in the dark – How cold it is!
The plumber has laid on running water

From the spring above the road – water, water,
That has to flow in the furrows of the garden,

That has to wash dishes, pots, old muddy clothes,
That has to be added to porridge or coffee

Before we can eat or drink – water is the sign of God,
Common, indispensable, easy to overlook –

How cold it is! Death will kill the cold
With one last stab, they say, and bring us to the sun-bright fields
                                                              of Canaan,

But I must stay outside till the last of nga mokai
Straggle in – time then to soak myself in the hot springs of Heaven!

1971 *1971*

The Ikons

Hard, heavy, slow, dark,
Or so I find them, the hands of Te Whaea

Teaching me to die. Some lightness will come later
When the heart has lost its unjust hope

For special treatment. Today I go with a bucket
Over the paddocks of young grass,

So delicate like fronds of maidenhair,
Looking for mushrooms. I find twelve of them,

Most of them little, and some eaten by maggots,
But they'll do to add to the soup. It's a long time now

Since the great ikons fell down,
God, Mary, home, sex, poetry,

Whatever one uses as a bridge
To cross the river that only has one beach,

And even one's name is a way of saying –
'This gap inside a coat' – the darkness I call God,

The darkness I call Te Whaea, how can they translate
The blue calm evening sky that a plane tunnels through

Like a little wasp, or the bucket in my hand,
Into something else? I go on looking

For mushrooms in the field, and the fist of longing
Punches my heart, until it is too dark to see.

1971 *1971*

Song for Sakyamuni

1

Loose as the washed pants and blouses that flap
On the thin wire they've tied round the corner post of the veranda,

My words are no longer the words of Apollo
But the river in its high gorges, life and death together,

Or the river in its shallows, mud and broken timber –
The body is a wound, Sakyamuni said,

Covered with damp skin, oozing out foul juice
From seven orifices, the wound we must bandage each day

In order to act and live in the light of the *Dharma*,
And my wound is half my trouble – the other half

Is the folly of believing I am I
In spite of contradiction – How hard to stop imitating

That waterlogged bee I saw on a clover head this morning,
Clinging to its red petals while the winter rain crashed down!

2

A thread can hold the bird back from rising
Just as well as a domed wire cage;

My loves, I grant, are all self-love,
Except for the love I cannot call my own,

The wind that moves in the branches of the tree
Without premeditation – Can the stomach never vomit up

Those broken bits of mushroom, the poisoned food of Yama? –
'I am, I am, I am,

'A poet, a Catholic, a dry alcoholic,
A man of forty-four' – you, Jesus, you, Sakyamuni,

Help me out of the pit! No ladder is necessary;
Ladders are part of the pit – my brothers, when the minute comes,

You will not see me; I will have gone out through the crack in
the rock
Like an old lizard – No more, no more, no more Becoming!

3

There was a man who lived at Jerusalem,
He had an old coat, he wore his toenails long,

The newspapers made up stories about him
To entertain the housewives – why couldn't he live

In the Kingdom of Anxiety like any other man
And go into his house like a rabbit to its burrow?

God was his problem; God and the universe;
He had, let us say, a problem of identity –

Now, if you go to the valley of Jerusalem,
You'll find that the silence is like any other silence,

You'll find that the river is like any other river,
You'll find that the rain is like any other rain,

But the old man has gone out of the picture,
Leaving an empty picture frame.

1971 *1976*

from *He Waiata mo taku Tangi*

for Eugene

1

At the beginning of March,
nineteen-seventy-one,
I'll open, if you like,
my guts for the world to see,
having nothing to lose,
not even hat or shoes, –
wife, home, reputation,
that too is gone, –

and if just after light
I go by the riverside
to eat the dusty fruit
from a bush of blackberry,
or wash my cut feet,
or kneel and meditate,
don't suppose it comes
from a cloudburst of sanctity!

My days go past like smoke,
my soul has long since grown
blind as an old opossum
in the roof of a Maori church, –
I think of the Cistercians
I met at Kopua,
God-loving Irishmen
with faces like children, –

Yes, they're my brothers, man,
because God makes me poor
and drives me out to walk
on the road to Wanganui
with an old coat and bare feet

and convent beads at my belt,
but I'm a madman
and the monks are sane men!

My father has followed his plough
into the darkest paddock, –
my mother is growing old
with Christ for company,
she won't last for ever, –
friend after friend has gone
into Te Whiro's hut
whose doors are made of stone, –

and like a man who rakes
for the live ones in a plague pit,
I do what I can, –
politeness, chastity,
or even a clean shirt,
are a great luxury
for one who throws his heart
for the mad to feed on, –

and I don't count how many
have climbed in the sack with me,
girls out of the bin
or those whose bodies stink
of lush or amphetamine,
to hide a muddled head
underneath my beard, –
may Christ have mercy

on us when we die! –
the tribe of nga mokai
who can do nothing well, –
may he keep us out of Hell
and bring us to the place
where the Maori corn grows green,
not for what we have done
but because we wanted peace!

Men out of the clink
come here and share their kai
at Hiruharama
in the coil of the taniwha, –
when mouths are peeled by thirst
they have to get water,
it is good to see them come,
the burnt and the lame, –

but my own soul one day
will lie in the dust
like a dead cicada, –
God makes a man,
we give him a name,
he goes back into the womb
of the earth and is lost,
unless God lifts the stone!

One tooth is left only
at the back of my bottom jaw,
there's kapok in my beard,
my guts are shrunk with fasting
among the Tama Toa,
I don't get sleep, –
this body falls to bits
like a mattress that gapes open, –

it would be nothing, man,
if the soul burned softly,
like a candle that's lit
in a windowless whare
to give us good dreams, –
but if I come to God
it will be by a road
where there's not even starlight, –

only the voice of rivers,
Rakaia, Rangitata,
Ohau, Clutha,
and now the Wanganui
who washes my body
before its burial,
will say nga karakia
mo Hemi te tutua,

the one who has become
a gap in a wall, –
like holy mothers
who speak for the child
who has lost his breath and voice
under the waterfall, –
and if they hold a tangi
at the wharepuni,

a river stone will do
well enough to hide
what lacks identity,
the kumara they throw
across the fence to rot
in the middle of the brambles
when the clean red ones are gathered
to cook in the hangi, –

and my wife Te Kare
is the one I give
stone, seed, breath, blood,
because Te Atua
joined us together, –
may she be the bird
on a branch by the river
who sings in joy for ever.

1971 *1979*

He Waiata mo Te Kare

1

Up here at the wharepuni
That star at the kitchen window
Mentions your name to me.

Clear and bright like running water
It glitters above the rim of the range,
You in Wellington,
I at Jerusalem,

Woman, it is my wish
Our bodies should be buried in the same grave.

2

To others my love is a plaited kono
Full or empty,
With chunks of riwai,
Meat that stuck to the stones.

To you my love is a pendant
Of inanga greenstone,
Too hard to bite,
Cut from a boulder underground.

You can put it in a box
Or wear it over your heart.

One day it will grow warm,
One day it will tremble like a bed of rushes
And say to you with a man's tongue,
'Taku ngakau ki a koe!'

3

I have seen at evening
Two ducks fly down
To a pond together.

The whirring of their wings
Reminded me of you.

4

At the end of our lives
Te Atua will take pity
On the two whom he divided.

To the tribe he will give
Much talking, te pia and a loaded hangi.

To you and me he will give
A whare by the seashore
Where you can look for crabs and kina
And I can watch the waves
And from time to time see your face
With no sadness,
Te Kare o Nga Wai.

5

No rafter paintings,
No grass-stalk panels,
No Maori mass,

Christ and his Mother
Are lively Italians
Leaning forward to bless,

No taniko band on her head,
No feather cloak on his shoulder,

No stairway to heaven,
No tears of the albatross.

Here at Jerusalem
After ninety years
Of bungled opportunities,
I prefer not to invite you
Into the pakeha church.

6

Waves wash on the beaches.
They leave a mark for only a minute.
Each grey hair in my beard
Is there because of a sin,

The mirror shows me
An old tuatara,
He porangi, he tutua,
Standing in his dusty coat.

I do not think you wanted
Some other man.
I have walked barefoot from the tail of the fish to the nose
To say these words.

7

Hilltop behind hilltop,
A mile of green pungas
In the grey afternoon
Bow their heads to the slanting spears of rain.

In the middle room of the wharepuni
Kat is playing the guitar, –
'Let it be! Let it be!'

Don brings home a goat draped round his shoulders.
Tonight we'll eat roasted liver.

One day, it is possible,
Hoani and Hilary might join me here,
Tired of the merry-go-round.

E hine, the door is open,
There's a space beside me.

8

Those we knew when we were young,
None of them have stayed together,
All their marriages battered down like trees
By the winds of a terrible century.

I was a gloomy drunk.
You were a troubled woman.
Nobody would have given tuppence for our chances,
Yet our love did not turn to hate.

If you could fly this way, my bird,
One day before we both die,
I think you might find a branch to rest on.

I chose to live in a different way.

Today I cut the grass from the paths
With a new sickle,
Working till my hands were blistered.

I never wanted another wife.

9

Now I see you conquer age
As the prow of a canoe beats down
The plumes of Tangaroa.

You, straight-backed, a girl,
Your dark hair on your shoulders,
Lifting up our grandchild,

How you put them to shame,
All the flouncing girls!

Your face wears the marks of age
As a warrior his moko,
Double the beauty,
A soul like the great albatross

Who only nests in mid ocean
Under the eye of Te Ra.

You have broken the back of age.
I tremble to see it.

10

Taraiwa has sent us up a parcel of smoked eels
With skins like fine leather.
We steam them in the colander.
He tells us the heads are not for eating,

So I cut off two heads
And throw them out to Archibald,
The old tomcat. He growls as he eats
Simply because he's timid.

Earlier today I cut thistles
Under the trees in the graveyard,

And washed my hands afterwards,
Sprinkling the sickle with water.

That's the life I lead,
Simple as a stone,
And all that makes it less than good, Te Kare,
Is that you are not beside me.

1972 1972

from *Autumn Testament*

1

As I come down the hill from Toro Poutini's house
My feet are sore, being bare, on the sharp stones

And that is a suitable penance. The dust of the pa road
Is cool, though, and I can see

The axe of the moon shift down behind the trees
Very slowly. The red light from the windows

Of the church has a ghostly look, and in
This place ghosts are real. The bees are humming loudly

In moonlight in their old hive above the church door
Where I go in to kneel, and come out to make my way

Uphill past a startled horse who plunges in the paddock
Above the nunnery. Now there are one or two

Of the tribe back in the big house – What would you have me do,
King Jesus? Your games with me have turned me into a boulder.

2

Wahi Ngaro, the void from which all life comes,
Has given us these woven spider-cages

That tie together the high heads of grass,
A civilisation in each. A stick can rip the white silk,

But that is not what I will do, having learnt
With manhood mercy, if no other good,

Two thousand perhaps in the tribe of nga mokai
Scattered like seeds now in the bins and the jails

Or occupied at their various occasions
Inside the spider-cage of a common dream,

Drugs, work, money. Siân, Kat,
Don and Francie, here with me at home

In the wharepuni – One great white flower
Shakes in the wind, turning a blind head towards our verandah.

4

Wahi Ngaro, the gap from which our prayers
Fall back like the toi-toi arrows

Children shoot upwards – Wahi Ngaro,
The limitless, the silent, the black night sky

From which the church huddles like a woman
On her hillock of ground – into your wide arms

Travelling, I forget the name of God,
Yet I can hear the flies roam through the rooms

Now at midday, feel the wind that flutters
The hippie goddess picture somebody painted

On an old blind and nailed on the wall. I can see
The orange flowers withering in a milk bottle,

Taste my tobacco phlegm, touch, if I like, the great bronze Christ
Theodore put up, on the poles of a cross he cut and bound himself.

5

Wahi Ngaro, now the ego like a sentry
At the gate of the soul closes its eyelids

For a moment, as today when
A crowd of ducks rose flapping at the place

Above the rapids where I go to bathe
Naked, splashing the water on my thighs,

And later I walked barefoot over the smooth boulders,
Thinking, 'There need be no other Heaven

'Than this world' – but rain spat soon
Out of a purple cloud, and I hid under

The willow leaves and bramble, as Adam did
Once from the Father. I brought back for Francie

A sprig of wet wild mint
That should go well tomorrow with the potatoes.

6

The darkness of oneself returns
Now that the house is empty,

A sense of danger in the room half dark,
Half lighted, seen through a squarish doorway,

Sticky rings left by cups on the table,
Darkness, the flutter of a moth,

A table spread in a tomb for the dead to eat at, –
That's it, the Dead! – 'Why did you pay

'A visit to Toro at night? Night is the time for the morepork,'
Wehe told me today, as we sat down to

Fried Maori bread, meat and pickle,
We who will certainly each of us one day return

To our mother the grave. The darkness of oneself
Comes from knowing nothing can be possessed.

9

Groper with throats like buckets,
Lazy swimming greenbone,

The rippling bulk of the stingray,
The mother shark and her young ones,

Quartz-eyed barracouta,
The iron legs of the kina,

The tribes of the octopus,
Fat flesh of the terakihi,

These images rise in sleep
Through the waters of my soul, –

As if I had been carried as a foetus
On the breast of Tangaroa,

And held in my heart an old hunger
To be dissolved and swallowed up by the waters.

10

The mossgrown haloed cross that crowns this church
Is too bleak for the mind of old Odysseus

Coming home to his table of rock, surviving and not surviving
Storms, words, axes, and the fingers of women,

Or the mind of Maui, who climbed inside the body
Of his ancestress and died there. Those who ride up river

In cars or the jetboat, see that high cross lifted
Above the low roofs of Jerusalem,

And speak of Mother Aubert and the Catholic Mission,
But when I see the sun fall and the moon rise

Over the edge of the ranges, I know what I have heard –
'The thoughts of a man's mind are many and secret' –

To the grass of the graveyard or a woman's breast
We turn in our pain for absolution.

11

At times when I walk beside the budding figtree
Or on the round stones by the river,

I meet the face of my dead father
With one or two white bristles on his chin

The safety razor missed. When he was younger
He'd hold the cut-throat with the ivory handle

And bring it with one deft stroke down his jowl,
Leaving the smooth blue skin. 'Old man,' I say,

'Long loved by me, still loved by many,
Is there a chance your son will ever join you

'In the kingdom of the summer stars?' He leaves me
Without a word, but like a touch behind him,

Greener the bulge of fruit among the figleaves,
Hotter the bright eye of the noonday sun.

14

Soon I will go South to my nephew's wedding
To the quiet land I came from,

Where all the ancestors are underground
And my father now among them. On my mother's wall

The picture Theo Schoon once painted
Shows him as the Iron Duke

With lines around his chin and mouth
Carved by the ploughshare. So he did look

In the time when a Labour Government planted my brother
On the Hautu prison farm for five years

For walking in my father's footprint
And refusing to carry a gun. Now in my mother's house

The picture is an icon. Father, is it easier to fight
The military machine, or the maggots of one's own heart?

Somebody in my dream was shaking a blanket
Sending a gust of wind with dust and fleas

Over my body – and when I woke,
In the dark room I saw a wavering shape

Like a vampire in a castle in the stories
I used to read as a boy. Whether or not it came

From the graveyard forty feet away
From the house corner, fear increases the strength

Of any kehua – so I crossed over and switched on the light,
Smoked a cigarette, chewed over a few pages

Of Peter Marin, and began to write this poem,
Since a man who'll die some day should hardly fear the dead,

And the tribe need a father who is afraid only
Of ceasing to love them well.

22

To pray for an easy heart is no prayer at all
Because the heart itself is the creaking bridge

On which we cross these Himalayan gorges
From bluff to bluff. To sweat out the soul's blood

Midnight after midnight is the ministry of Jacob,
And Jacob will be healed. This body that shivers

In the foggy cold, tasting the sour fat,
Was made to hang like a sack on its thief's cross,

Counting it better than bread to say the words of Christ,
'*Eli! Eli!*' The Church will be shaken like a

Blanket in the wind, and we are the fleas that fall
To the ground for the dirt to cover. Brother thief,

You who are lodged in my ribcage, do not rail at
The only gate we have to paradise.

25

Richard will not come here, the shy one,
Wary as a crayfish whose feelers jut out

From a crevice in the rock. When he was thirteen,
In the maths class, his teacher used to stand him

In a wastepaper basket at the front of the room,
And once I heard the lawyer ask him,

'Can't you think of something better to do with your life?'
'No.' The face like a young stone mask:

'Idiots have no opinions.'
I heard him breaking bottles in the street

The night Naomi turned him down;
Naomi was a mother who had found him

Too hard to carry. Yet he broke no windows.
It hurts me to watch the snaring of the unicorn.

27

When I stayed those three months at Macdonald Crescent
In the house of Lazarus, three tribes were living

In each of the storeys – on the ground floor, the drunks
Who came there when the White Lodge burnt down;

Above them, the boobheads; and scattered between the first
And second storey, the students who hoped to crack

The rock of education. The drunks are my own tribe.
One Sunday, the pubs being shut, they held a parliament

In the big front room – Lofty with his walking stick,
Phil the weeper, Taffy who never spoke much,

And one or two others – in conclave they sat, like granite columns
Their necks, like Tritons their faces,

Like tree-roots their bodies. Sober as Rhadamanthus
They judged the town and found it had already been judged.

29

I think the Lord on his axe-chopped cross
Is laughing as usual at my poems,

My solemn metaphors, my ladder-climbing dreams,
For he himself is incurably domestic,

A family man who never lifted a sword,
An only son with a difficult mother,

If you understand my thought. He has saddled me again
With the cares of a household, and no doubt

Has kept me away from Otaki
Because I'd spout nonsense, and wear my poverty

As a coat of vanity. Down at the Mass
Today, as Francie told me to, I took Communion

For her (and Siân as well) cursing gently
The Joker who won't let me shuffle my own pack.

31

I tell the girls, 'After long meditation,
Scrutiny of books in Arabic and Latin,

'Consultation (by telephone) with twenty-five colleagues,
Examination with bioscope and xylophone,

'I have come to the crux of my diagnosis,
Your ailment is a hybrid,

'Tuberculosis, cholera, leprosy,
In one package' – they are not impressed,

Nor, I think, is the master of the house,
The Maori sergeant from the First World War

In uniform, seated on a cane chair
In the foot-high photograph upon our mantelpiece.

I think he has summed us up – 'Kaore nga pukapuka!
You might stay well if you learnt Maoritanga.'

33

'Mother, your statue by the convent path
Has chips of plaster scattered round it

'Where rain or frost have stripped you of your mantle – '
'It doesn't matter.' 'As you know, in winter

'I often kneel there under the knife-edged moon
Praying for – ' 'I hear those prayers.'

'Mother, your blue gown seems like stone,
Too rigid – ' 'What they make of me

'Is never what I am.' 'Our Church looks to the young
Like a Medusa; they want to be – '

'Free, yes; Christ is the only Master.'
'They are taught to judge themselves.' 'Suffer it.'

'But sin – ' 'I see no sin. My secret is
I hold the Child I was given to hold.'

36

This fine windy morning I think about
The leper lying beside the fruitstalls in Calcutta

Under the shade of the great bridge. The oil-stained bandages
Around his limbs, the flies moving slowly

In and out of his nostrils, over his eyelids;
That lion face of dark mahogany

Turned up its brow to the overlying cloud
Behind which Rahm might live, from which a few spots

Of rain aspersed the pavement. I threw some coins
Into his tin dish. The policeman, built like a Maori,

Guarding the fruitstalls in his khaki shorts,
Said, 'They're no use to him.' But the man was not quite dead.

When he was younger he should have had a gun.
There or in Karori, the sickness is, not to be wanted.

The centre of our dreaming is the cave
That the world translates as brothel. Margaret told me once

A dream she had, about a house
In a meadow by the sea, old and full of passages,

Upstair and downstair rooms where the tribe were sleeping,
And three great waves came out of the sea

And washed around the house and left it standing,
Though for a while they had hidden the sun and the moon.

There has to be, I think, some shelter,
A home, an all–but–God, an all–but–mother

In time and place, not just the abstract void
Of I looking for me. Around these walls

They dipped their hands in paint and left their handprints
As on the walls of caves the Magdalenian hunters.

42

The rata blooms explode, the bow–legged tomcat
Follows me up the track, nipping at my ankle,

The clematis spreads her trumpet, the grassheads rattle
Ripely, drily, and all this

In fidelity to death. Today when Father Te Awhitu
Put on the black gown with the silver cross,

It was the same story. The hard rind of the ego
Won't ever crack except to the teeth of Te Whiro,

That thin man who'll eat the stars. I can't say
It pleases me. In the corner I can hear now

The high whining of a mason fly
Who carries the spiders home to his house

As refrigerated meat. 'You bugger off,' he tells me,
'Your Christianity won't put an end to death.'

44

This testament, a thing of rags and patches,
Will end soon. I cannot say, like Villon,

'Pray for me and for yourselves,'
For this is another century. That poor man ate his lunch

With the corpses of streetboys hanging overhead
And was part owner of some kind of brothel,

But the harps and lutes of paradise on the church wall
Were just as real as the bogs of fire,

The burghers sweated in their high fur gowns,
The slaves lay down to sleep on a straw mattress,

And most of it made sense. As if God had opened
A crack in the rock of the world to let some daylight in,

Saying, 'Be poor like Me.' Our life is the one
We make in darkness for ourselves.

45

Tomorrow I'll go down to Wellington,
Hitching, if I'm lucky, a ride down the river road

Past the karaka trees and the town houses
That turn the river into the Wanganui ditch

With shit that floats upstream below the bridges
When the tide pushes home. I'll go then

Southward among the sad green farms
Where the sheep get more freedom than their masters,

Past beaches with the plumes of toetoe blowing
In a wind that only Maori kids on horses

Can bargain with, down, down the straight coast road
To the dream city, the old fat sow

Who smothers her children. I'll wear no diving suit
And sit cross-legged in a pub doorway.

46

After writing for an hour in the presbytery
I visit the church, that dark loft of God,

And make my way uphill. The grass is soaking my trousers,
The night dark, the rain falling out of the night,

And the old fears walk side by side with me,
Either the heavy thump of an apple

Hitting the ground, or the creaking of the trees,
Or the presence of two graveyards,

The new one at the house, the old one on the hill
That I have never entered. Heaven is light

And Hell is darkness, so the Christmen say,
But this dark is the belly of the whale

In which I, Jonah, have to make my journey
Till the fear has gone. Fear is the only enemy.

48

The spider crouching on the ledge above the sink
Resembles the tantric goddess,

At least as the Stone Age people saw her
And carved her on their dolmens. Therefore I don't kill her,

Though indeed there is a simpler reason,
Because she is small. Kehua, vampire, eight-eyed watcher

At the gate of the dead, little Arachne, I love you,
Though you hang your cobwebs up like dirty silk in the hall

And scuttle under the mattress. Remember I spared your children
In their cage of white cloth you made as an aerial castle,

And you yourself, today, on the window ledge.
Fear is the only enemy. Therefore when I die,

And you wait for my soul, you hefty as a king crab
At the door of the underworld, let me pass in peace.

1972 *1972*

Te Whiore o te Kuri

1

Two trucks pass me in a cloud of dust
As I come up the road from the river,

So I put the bathing towel over my mouth
And breathe damp cloth. Taraiwa on the old bridge

Is cutting the iron struts with a blow torch,
But he tells me – 'Kua mutu' – 'The oxygen is finished.'

I climb the long track to the wharepuni,
Meditating on the words of Thomas Merton –

'At the end of life God presses down a seal
On the wax of the soul. If the wax is warm

'It receives the mark; if not, it is crushed to powder' –
So be it. My own heart may yet be my coffin.

Up here they give me a cup of crushed apple pulp
To drink. In autumn the kai falls from the trees.

2

The dark light shines from the graves of the saints,
By which I mean the humble ones

Buried beside our house and under the bramble
That hides the fallen pas where sheep are grazing

And leave their clots of wool. The dark light shines
At the heart of the tangi where a tent has been put up

To hold the coffin, and a widow with a
Three-day-sleepless face is waiting for the

Resurrection. I remember
When the church was shut at Ngaruawahia,

Kneeling instead in front of the stone statue
Of Te Whaea, darkened by rain, eroded by moss,

Under an apple tree. The dark light shines
Wherever the humble have opened a door for it.

3

A giant weta climbs the curling ladder
Of the scrim beside my bed. I don't want

The scratching of this amateur bush demon
Interfering with my dreams,

Or love-bites on my neck. First Steve comes through
With a saw – 'To cut him in half,' he says –

Then Zema – 'You're piss-poor, Hemi,
At killing' (she giggles) – but I get a shoe

From the other room, stand on the strongest chair,
Wield it by the toe and belt him – crack!

The weta, trailing white guts, drops to the floor,
A three-inch dragon in his broken armour,

Poor creature! I finish him off with another blow
And lie back to read while the mosquitoes play their flutes.

4

The rain falls all day. Now the tanks will be full.
The road down river will turn to wet porridge

And the slips begin. Herewini told me
How Te Atua warned him that the bank would fall,

So he left the grader and came to shift his mates, –
They ran to safety and the bank did fall

Silently, eighty tons of earth and boulders,
Burying him to the armpits. His leg is still blue

Where the great stone cracked it and the bolts were put through
                                                        the bone,
But he can walk on it. The drips from the holes in the roof

Spatter in the kitchen, on the boards behind the stove,
At the foot of Francie's bed. Beyond the lid of cloud

I hear the droning of the birds of Armageddon
That one day will end the world we understand.

5

The tribe in their own time are making a fowl run
Below the big chestnut. Therefore I wake

To hear the screech of nails being dragged with hammers
At the front of the house – Steve and Gregg

Doing what once would hardly happen
In two years. One by one the girls

Come in to visit their old hairy koro
On the broad of his back in a sleeping bag

Resting his rheumatism – Te Huinga,
Zema, Francie, Cam, they bring in coffee,

But stay to sit and open out their thoughts
And put their heads on my pillow. Some people think

I keep a harem. No; my back's not strong enough.
I keep a chook pen for birds of paradise.

6

'Te whiore o te kuri' – this is the tail of the dog
That wags at the end of my book;

After a dispute with one dear Maori friend
I walk all night on the road to Raetihi,

Thinking, 'Twenty-four miles will pulp the pads of my feet
Till the soles of them swell up like balloons;

'Pain in my feet; pain of my hara.' This morning
I saw the sun rise molten and red

Over the hill at Herewini's house
At Raetihi. But staggering on the stones

Last night, I had to stop, and looked up at the stars
And saw those ribs of white fire

Hung there like the underside of punga leaves
Planted for our human shelter.

7

To go forward like a man in the dark
Is the meaning of this dark vocation;

So simple, tree, star, the bare cup of the hills,
The lifelong grave of waiting

As indeed it has to be. To ask for Jacob's ladder
Would be to mistake oneself and the dark Master,

Yet at times the road comes down to a place
Where water runs and horses gallop

Behind a hedge. There it is possible to sit,
Light a cigarette, and rub

Your bruised heels on the cold grass. Always because
A man's body is a meeting house,

Ribs, arms, for the tribe to gather under,
And the heart must be their spring of water.

1972 *1972*

from *Letter to Peter Olds*

4

The revolution doesn't need guns;
It happens whenever a man arrested for being

Out of work, and booted into the meat wagon,
Begins to laugh instead of squaring his fists;

It happens whenever a screw in Paremoremo
Walks out of his job instead of standing and watching

Twenty men bumming a boy. It happens
When the owner of the restaurant sits down with a moneyless
                                                    customer

To pass the time of day. It happened for me
Lately at Taumarunui, when I stood on the grass of the marae

Beside one kuia, and said to her,
'When I am beside you I know that the earth below

'My feet is our mother. It gives me a sense of peace.'
The revolution happens when the eyes begin to open at last.

1972 1972

from *Five Sestinas*

1   Winter in Jerusalem

The *I Ching* tells me *T'ai*, the sign of peace,
Is what I venture in. The pungas on the hill,
So lately loaded with snow, are green again
Though some branches were broken. Where many men gather
From need or friendship, truth begins to waken
As eels rise in the dark river.

If Heaven gives me this old house by a river,
It is not for myself, but for the purpose of peace,
As the thunder and rain of spring make green things waken,
A fence of poplar leaves between us and the hill
Who is our mother, or the chestnuts we gather
In autumn when the earth is warm again.

In our dreams it may happen the dead return again,
As if the earth spoke to us, because time is a river
On whose bank in ignorance the tribes gather
With emblems of battle, yet desiring peace.
The fathers instruct us from their holy hill
So that the warrior souls may waken.

In winter with a heavy mind I waken
And wait for the sun to lift the fogs again
That bind Jerusalem. Like a bridegroom above the hill
He touches with hands of fire the waves of the river
Like the body of a woman. Our words are words of peace
In this house where the wounded children gather.

We can go out with Maori kits to gather
Watercress, or some tough lads who waken
Early will break the veil of peace
With gunshots, combing the bush again
For young goats, or lift the eel-trap from the river
As fog shifts from the highest hill.

The times are like some rough and roadless hill
We have to climb. I do not hope to gather
Pears in winter, or halt the flow of the river
That buries in sludge the souls who begin to waken
And know themselves. Our peace can't patch again
The canoe that is broken, yet all men value peace.

Peace is the language of the pungas on the hill
Not growing for any gain. These images I gather
As eels waken in the darkness of the river.

3   The Dark Welcome

In the rains of winter the pa children
Go in gumboots on the wet grass. Two fantails clamber
On stems of bramble and flutter their wings
In front of me, indicating a visit
Or else a death. Below the wet marae
They wait in a transport shelter for the truck to come,

Bringing tobacco, pumpkins, salt. The kai will be welcome
To my hungry wandering children
Who drink at the springs of the marae
And find a Maori ladder to clamber
Up to the light. The cops rarely visit,
Only the fantails flutter their wings

Telling us about the dark angel's wings
Over a house to the north where a man has come
Back from Wellington, to make a quiet visit,
Brother to one of the local children,
Because the boss's scaffolding was too weak to clamber
Up and down, or else he dreamt of the marae

When the car was hitting a bend. Back to the marae
He comes, and the fantails flutter their wings,
And the children at the tangi will shout and clamber
Over trestles, with a noise of welcome,
And tears around the coffin for one of the grown-up children
Who comes to his mother's house on a visit,

Their town cousin, making a longer visit,
To join the old ones on the edge of the marae
Whose arms are bent to cradle their children
Even in death, as the pukeko's wings
Cover her young. The dark song of welcome
Will rise in the meeting house, like a tree where birds clamber,

Or the Jacob's-ladder where angels clamber
Up and down. Thus the dead can visit
The dreams and words of the living, and easily come
Back to shape the deeds of the marae,
Though rain falls to wet the fantail's wings
As if the earth were weeping for her children.

Into the same canoe my children clamber
From the wings of the iron hawk and the Vice Squad's visit
On the knees of the marae to wait for what may come.

1972 *1974*

Sestina of the River Road

I want to go up the river road
Even by starlight or moonlight
Or no light at all, past the Parakino bridge,
Past Atene where the tarseal ends,
Past Koroniti where cattle run in a paddock,
Past Operiki, the pa that was never taken,

Past Matahiwi, Ranana, till the last step is taken
And I can lie down at the end of the road
Like an old horse in his own paddock
Among the tribe of Te Hau. Then my heart will be light
To be in the place where the hard road ends
And my soul can walk the rainbow bridge

That binds earth to sky. In his cave below the bridge,
Where big eels can be taken
With the hinaki, and the ends
Of willow branches trail from the edge of the road
Onto the water, the dark one rises to the light,
The taniwha who guards the tribal paddock

And saves men from drowning. Down to Poutini's paddock
The goats come in winter, and trucks cross the bridge
In the glitter of evening light
Loaded with coils of wire, five dogs, and wood they have taken
From a rotten fence. On the bank above the road
At the marae my journey ends

Among the Maori houses. Indeed when my life ends
I hope they find room in the paddock
Beside the meeting house, to put my bones on a road
That goes to the Maori dead. A gap I cannot bridge,
Here in the town, like a makutu has taken
Strength from my body and robbed my soul of light,

Because this blind porangi gets his light
From Hiruharama. The darkness never ends
In Pharaoh's kingdom. God, since you have taken
Man's flesh, grant me a hut in the Maori paddock
To end my life in, with their kindness as my bridge,
Those friends who took me in from the road

Long ago. Their tears are the road of light
I need to bridge your darkness when the world ends.
To the paddock of Te Whiti let this man be taken.

1972 *1979*

Sestina of the Makutu

In the dream I am lost in a Maori graveyard
Among the dunes of sand,
And like a wave of black water
The makutu hits me. No terror like this,
Latrines, ovens, graves, a woman's anger
Splitting my skull with a stone axe,

Yet it is Te Whiro who wields the axe
Or else te taipo, the masters of the boneyard
Where I have to walk. Why should the Maori anger
Rise from the roots of the grass and the sand
To choke the soul of this
Old pakeha? To drown in deep water

Is the fate of those who go into the water
Of the marae. I know why the axe
Is raised above my skull. I know why this
Dream comes out of Te Whiro's yard
To flatten a house built on sand
With the storm of an old anger,

And I accept the anger
As drowning men open their lungs to the water
Because the battle among the dunes of sand
Is won by losing it. I know the axe
Of the makutu was made in a yard
Where warriors drank black water before this

For their mother the land. The towns built over this
Black bog of a people's anger,
Sweat-shop, jail and railway yard,
Will fall like leaves into the water
When willows are chopped by the farmer's axe.
Blood swallowed by the sand

Rises again out of the sand.
On an old pakeha's head let this
Makutu break its axe,
Since anger breeds anger.
The one who walked the water
Has no voice in Te Whiro's yard

Except that the yard's dark sand
Should drink down like water this
Old man's blood, and aroha, not anger, blunt the axe.

1972 *1976*

The Tiredness of Me and Herakles

a letter to Herman Gladwin

1

I trapped the great boar,
A Jansenist priest in his lair.
His tusks were longer than the Auckland Harbour Bridge,
His logic pure as the seafoam,
'All men are damned except myself.
The christly do not have erections.'
The occasion of our dispute was a teen-age chick
To whom I had written a poem.
Though he booted me out of his presbytery
We parted civilly enough.
I asked him for a conditional blessing.

2

The cleansing of the stables
Took twelve thousand tons of river water.
The horseshit had hardened in the stalls like concrete.
You couldn't shift it with a pick or shovel.
Ritualism, fetichism, moralism,
Simplicism, angelism, dualism,
Drayload after drayload went swirling out the door.
I was afraid nothing would be left.
But when the floor was wet and cool as limestone
I found wedged in a crack one iron crucifix
And a thin medal of Our Lady.

3

The sky met the earth
To the west of that marae.
Great trees hung over the meeting house.
The earth giant did not greet me gladly.
'Apples,' he grumbled, 'too many apples,
My troubles began with an apple.'
But he let me take the rigid weight
Of the firmament on the strap-hardened shoulder
I got as a city postman long ago.
The apple that he plucked from the oldest tree
Burned in his hand like a sun.

4

In the battle with the shield-bearing women
I got this wound that makes me limp a little,
An arrow lodged one centimetre
Above the right testicle.
They cut one breast off to draw back the bowstring,
The other breast they keep to feed their children.
'Pornographer,' they shouted, 'you have poisoned the wells!'
The dust rose on a desert whirlwind.
Their queen Hippolyta grew amorous
After defeat. I did not like her.
She smelt of dexedrine and cabbage water.

5

All day I ploughed with savage oxen
That snorted and farted like runaway tractors.
That was the labour involving the printed rubbish
Plain men use at evening to wrap up fish and oysters
Or at midday as a table cloth.
The king was gloomy when the paddock had been ploughed,
Though the furrows lay like polished metal.

'You are in danger of becoming vain,' he said,
'With too much exposure by the mass media.'
I noticed that the summer flies
Had laid their eggs in his beard.

6

The bout with Death was a hard one.
He wore a black uniform.
'Why don't you cut your hair?' he asked me.
'Life is filth. I keep the world clean.'
He had come with a pure heart from morning Mass
For a work-out at the police gymnasium
Before supervising the cleaning of a cell
That had some blood and vomit on its wall.
We wrestled in a fog of greyness
Till the swastika pin fell out of his shirt.
I was glad when the boss man called it off.

7

This wet October night
In a house in Auckland
The horseleech's daughter
Is crying, 'Give! Give!'
I have given her my fingers.
I have given her my liver to eat.
I have given her my skull to use as a soup bowl.
The ones who come here stoned on LSD
Forget they had a convent education.
To kill the heads of the hydra
You need a clever branding iron.

8

Three times in twenty years
I have wept a few tears.
I prefer laughter
But it gives me a hernia.
Herman, you old yelling shouting foetus,
Some wisdom has trickled through the cracks in my egg.
The drizzling grief of the town is the swag I carry.
A fist fight would improve the score.
I do not take my compass from Lenin.
My people rarely laugh or weep.
The fear of being hated has turned them into rock.

9

Today I smashed a green hydrangea bush
With a walking stick
At the edge of somebody's private lawn.
Every leaf was the head of a friend.
The meat wagon did not come to the scene.
Five labours still to go.
I am tired already.

1972 *1979*

Ode to Auckland

Auckland, you great arsehole,
Some things I like about you
Some things I cannot like.

I came to the Art School, carrying the paintings
Of an eighteen-year-old chick.
On the door of one room somebody had written 'Life'
But there was death inside it.

A skeleton hung there by a hook in its skull
Its ribs brown with earth, age, or varnish.
The statue of a Greek god lay on the floor
With his prick and balls knocked off by a chisel.
'Alison,' I said, 'they've buggered the god of death,
They've cut the balls off the god of love.
How can their art survive?'

'Roimata ua, roimata tangata – '
The tears of rain are falling,
Tears of rain, tears of men.

I went to Mass at Newman Hall,
Then visited the Varsity Cafeteria
With six Catholic acquaintances.
One wanted to show me the poems he had written,
One talked about the alternate society,
One wanted to convert the world,
One girl in glasses gave me the glad eye,
Another praised the pentecostal movement,
Another hoed into his plate of cheese and camel turds.

I said, 'Excuse me a minute, there's a Maori friend of mine,
If he doesn't get a place to crash tonight
The cops will pick him up for the four crimes
They dislike most in Auckland,
Not having a job,
Wearing old clothes,
Having long hair,
Above all, for being Maori.
When they shift him to the cells in the meat wagon
The last crime might earn him five punches in the gut.
Could any one of you give him a night's lodging?'

They were extremely sorry.
The bourgeois Christ began to blush on the Cross.
The Holy Spirit squawked and laid an egg.
One had landlord trouble,
One had to swot for exams,

One was already overcrowded,
One didn't know exactly,
One still wanted to show me the poems he had written,
And the last one still silently consumed his plate of camel turds.

I took the Maori lad to Keir Volkerling's place.
He slept on a mattress in the bathroom.
Keir was not a Christian, or a student.
He worked ten hours a day
Digging drains or mixing concrete
To support an average of twenty-five people
Who would otherwise have been in jail
For being out of work,
For wearing an old coat,
For having their hair down to their shoulders,
And above all, for the crime of being Maori.

Christianity has weakened my brain cells, brother,
I haven't got the fortitude of Keir Volkerling.
The Auckland Varsity gives me a pain in the rectum.
I am waiting for the day
When its wedding cake tower goes down in a pile of rubble
From a bomb planted by an intelligent boobhead
Or a not-so-intelligent Varsity radical.

The Auckland Art School gives me a pain in both my testicles.
They don't know the best of Illingworth.
They admire the worst of McCahon.
Why not burn the Art School down
And get some old houses and do a bit of painting
Either with a brush on the ceiling
Or with a brush on a bit of canvas?

I paid a visit to an old friend
Who used to write some good poems.
The door of his office was painted black and yellow,
The colour of the plague flag.

'Peter,' I asked him, 'could you spare me a dollar?'
He looked unhappy.
He was putting on some ceremonial robes
For a meeting of the University Council.
'I'm sorry, man,' I said,
'I didn't mean to interrupt you.'

Outside his office the wind rustled
Dead leaves on the concrete pavement.
I shook hands with an old moss-grown statue
And went barefoot down the road.

Auckland, even when I am well stoned
On a tab of LSD or on Indian grass
You still look to me like an elephant's arsehole
Surrounded with blue-black haemorrhoids.

The sound of the opening and shutting of bankbooks,
The thudding of refrigerator doors,
The ripsaw voices of Glen Eden mothers yelling at their children,
The chugging noise of masturbation from the bedrooms of the
                                        bourgeoisie,
The voices of dead teachers droning in dead classrooms,
The TV voice of Mr Muldoon,
The farting noise of the trucks that grind their way down Queen
                                        Street
Has drowned forever the song of Tangaroa on a thousand beaches,
The sound of the wind among the green volcanoes,
And the whisper of the human heart.

Boredom is the essence of your death,
I would take a trip to another town
Except that the other towns resemble you exactly.

How can I live in a country where the towns are made like coffins
And the rich are eating the flesh of the poor
Without even knowing it?

O Father Lenin, help us in our great need!
The people seem to enjoy building the pyramids.
Moses would get a mighty cold reception.
They'd kiss the arse of Pharaoh any day of the week

For a pat on the head and a dollar note.
At another time in another place
Among the Ngati-Whatua
When they brought the dead child into the meeting house

She opened her eyes and smiled.

18 October 1972 *1972*

[Moss on plum branches]

Moss on plum branches and
A soft rain falling – no other house
Spread out its arms around me
As this has done – I go
From here with a gap inside me where a world
Has been plucked from my entrails – fire and
Food, flowers and faces
Painted on walls – the voices of two friends
Recalling the always present paradise
We enter and cannot remain in.

Arohanui

Hemi

1972 *2001*

[A pair of sandals]

A pair of sandals, old black pants
And leather coat – I must go, my friends,
Into the dark, the cold, the first beginning
Where the ribs of the ancestor are the rafters
Of a meeting house – windows broken
And the floor white with bird dung – in there
The ghosts gather who will instruct me
And when the river fog rises
Te ra rite tonu te Atua –
The sun who is like the Lord
Will warm my bones, and his arrows
Will pierce to the centre of the shapeless clay of the mind.

Hemi.

1972 *2001*

NOTES, GLOSSARIES,
BIBLIOGRAPHY AND INDEXES

Notes on the Poems

Letter to Noel Ginn
Noel Ginn   a pacifist and poet sentenced to defaulter's detention and imprisoned with Baxter's older brother. Baxter and Ginn's four-year correspondence features in Millar, *Spark to a Waiting Fuse* (see bibliography).
Placarded Tubes   London's underground railway system, its walls lined with advertisements.
Cotswolds   from 1937 to 1938 Baxter attended Sibford School, a Quaker boarding school in the English Cotswolds (see 'School Days', p. 77).
bells of ling   the bell-shaped flowers of heather (Scots: ling).
Glencoe … the red-coats   the site of the infamous massacre on 13 February 1692 of members of the MacDonald clan by soldiers (red-coats) predominately from the Campbell-dominated Argyll regiment.

University Song
Written for the University of Otago. In MS Book 14: '*Tune*: Jerusalem'.

To my Father ['Today, looking at the flowering peach']
'in measure like a dancer'   see 'Little Gidding' by T.S. Eliot.

The Giant's Grave
Airt   (Scots) a cardinal point on the compass.

Reflections on a Varsity Career
Queen City of the South   Dunedin.
S.C.M.   the Student Christian Mission.
the Robert Burns and the Bowling Green   popular hotels in North Dunedin frequented by students.
Lane's Emulsion   a popular children's tonic in the early twentieth century invented by South Island chemist Edward Lane. Its ingredients included cod liver oil, creosote, lime and soda 'emulsified and made palatable' with fresh eggs.
saveloy skins   casings of dried red pork sausage, used here to mean condoms.
hard yacker   hard work.

Crossing Cook Strait
Seddon Richard John (Dick) Seddon (1845–1906). Liberal politician and Premier of New Zealand.
Savage Michael Joseph Savage (1872–1940), Prime Minister of the first Labour Government which in the mid-1930s created New Zealand's comprehensive social security system.

Harry Fat and Uncle Sam
Mazengarb Queen's Counsel Oswald Mazengarb was appointed in 1954 to chair the Special Committee on Moral Delinquency in Children and Adolescents. Its report blamed the perceived promiscuity of the nation's youth on the absence from home of working mothers, the easy availability of contraceptives, and on young women who enticed men into having sex.
Corbett E.B. Corbett, Minister for Māori Affairs in the early 1950s, at a time when the government's aim was to assimilate Māori into mainstream New Zealand life.

A Rope for Harry Fat
Te Whiu Edward Thomas Te Whiu was one of the last people to be hanged for murder in New Zealand. His 1955 execution gave impetus to the campaign to abolish capital punishment.

Husband to Wife
Koromex a vaginal spermicide.

By the Dry Cardrona
The Cardrona River flows down a steep valley in Central Otago. This poem is a song from Baxter's play *Jack Winter's Dream* (1956) and does not appear in any of the manuscript notebooks.

School Days
Refers to Sibford School in the English Cotswolds, which Baxter attended 1937–8.

Spring Song of a Civil Servant
Lions the visiting British rugby team.
Athletic Park Wellington rugby stadium, since demolished.

Election 1960
King Log Walter Nash, the Labour Prime Minister of New Zealand.
King Stork Keith Holyoake, the leader of the National Party.

To a Samoan Friend
A later version of this poem is included in the sequence 'Words to Lay a Strong Ghost' as poem no. 10, 'The Friend'. See *Collected Poems*, p. 361.

An Ode to the Reigning Monarch on the Occasion of Her Majesty's Visit to Pig Island
Bellamys   a restaurant for members of the New Zealand parliament.
Holyoake   See note to 'Election 1960', above.

Pig Island Letters
Pig Island   used 'with satirical nuance' by Baxter to refer to the whole of New Zealand.
Pig Island Letters, 1
Leith Stream   a small Dunedin river that flows through the University of Otago, where Baxter was briefly a student.
Pig Island Letters, 3
your book   Shadbolt's *Summer Fires and Winter Country*.
Pig Island Letters, 4
Remuera   Auckland's most exclusive suburb, employed by Baxter to represent Pākehā privilege and insularity.
Hunn report   1961 report by J.K. Hunn, Acting Secretary for Māori Affairs, ostensibly on the Department of Māori Affairs, but containing far-reaching recommendations on social reforms affecting the Māori people. In MS Book 24 Baxter calls it 'a gloomy and erroneous account of Māori social habits, commandeered by the Government to quiet the chronically bad conscience of its bureaucrats.'
Sea-eggs   see glossary, 'kina'.
Pig Island Letters, 5
the fish of Maui   a reference to the Māori myth that Te Ika a Māui, the North Island of New Zealand, was brought to the surface by Māui using an enchanted hook.
Pig Island Letters, 6
Fairburn   A.R.D. Fairburn (1904–57), a major New Zealand poet of the 1920s to 1950s.
Pig Island Letters, 6
moa   a large flightless, herbivorous bird, endemic to New Zealand, thought to have gone extinct around 1500CE. The biggest of the ten species reached about 3.7m in height and weighed about 230kg. Baxter's likening of the poet Fairburn to a 'great moa' is also an oblique reference to Allen Curnow's famous early poem 'The Skeleton of the Great Moa in the Canterbury Museum, Christchurch'.

Pig Island Letters, 9
Lowry   Bob Lowry, a colourful Auckland typographer, printer and publisher, and a strong supporter of many writers. He was renowned for haphazard business practices and the hosting of bohemian parties. His suicide in 1963 shook many in the literary community – Baxter being no exception.

Pig Island Letters, 11
Baiame   a creational ancestral hero in the dreaming of indigenous Australians of South-East Australia.
wirinun   a medicine man or wise man. In one account Wahn the Crow (who originally possessed human form) is cursed by Baiame for stealing fire and then refusing to share it with humans. The curse blackens his limbs, changing him from a man to a black bird.

Letter to Robert Burns
Octagon   the city centre of Dunedin.

The Old Earth Closet
Man Alone   a reference to the influential New Zealand novel by John Mulgan.

At Aramoana
Gea   Baxter preferred this archaic spelling for Gaia or Gaea, in ancient Greek mythology the goddess of the earth and mother of Cronus and the Titans.

The Maori Jesus
telling a dee   dee, junkie slang for a police detective.
Porirua   Porirua Hospital (originally Porirua Lunatic Asylum), north of Wellington, operated from 1887 to 2007 as one of New Zealand's major psychiatric hospitals.

Mother and Son
fantail   (Māori: pīwakawaka) a small, friendly, insect-eating bird which has a distinctive tail resembling a spread fan. See glossary, 'Hine-nui-te-pō'.

Fitz Drives Home the Spigot
pony beer   a small measure of beer in a glass of only 140 ml capacity.

Grandfather
chanter   the reed-like part of the bagpipe with finger holes upon which

the player creates the melody.

Reflections at Lowburn Ferry
obol an allusion to Charon's obol, the coin placed in or on the mouth of a dead person before burial.

Air Flight North
Nils Holgerssen the little boy in Swedish author Selma Lagerlöf's book *The Wonderful Adventures of Nils*, who is shrunk for tormenting animals and redeems himself through good deeds while flying over all the provinces of Sweden on the back of a goose.

Stephanie
This is poem 2 of a series of three written by Baxter to his five-week-old granddaughter.

For Hone
The Māori poet Hone Tuwhare (1922–2008).

Jerusalem Sonnets, 31
Moutoa Island up-river from present-day Wanganui city, the site of a fierce battle in May 1964 between Hauhau forces intent on attacking the Pākehā settlement and local Māori defenders.

Autumn Testament, 6
morepork (Māori: rurua) a native owl common throughout New Zealand in wooded areas including suburbs, roosting by day and active at night; the name mimics its cry.

Letter to Peter Olds, 4
Paremoremo a maximum security prison near Auckland.

Māori Glossary

The glossary of Māori words used by Baxter follows his non-macronised spellings (for a full explanation of the use of macrons in Māori spelling, see the note 'Words in Māori', p. xxii). However, I have, where appropriate, indicated the correct macronised form in square brackets at the beginning of a definition and indicated where some minor corrections to Baxter's usage would be appropriate (e.g. 'kōnae' for 'kono'). I have also expanded the definitions beyond those supplied by Baxter, based on P.M. Ryan's *Reed Dictionary of Modern Māori* (Auckland: Reed, 1995) and Te Whanake's superb on-line Māori dictionary at www.tewhanake.maori.nz.

Phrases beginning with the introductory words E, he, ka, ko, kua, nga and te are listed under the second word of the phrase.

a   and
Te Ariki   an ariki is a paramount chief or similar leading aristocratic individual. Baxter uses Te Ariki to refer to Christ 'the Lord'
aroha   love, affection, sympathy, charity, compassion, empathy
arohanui   a plenitude of aroha, with deep affection – often used in signing off letters to friends
atua   ancestor with continuing influence, god, demon, supernatural being, deity, ghost, object of superstitious regard, strange being, god
Te Atua   the Judaeo-Christian God

E   O, oh

haere ra   [haere rā] farewell, goodbye
hangi   [hāngī] an earth oven for cooking food with steam and heat from heated stones, or, by common usage, a feast
hara   sin, transgression
Hatana   [Hātana] Satan
te hau   the wind
he   a, some
hinaki   [hīnaki] an eel-trap, wicker eel basket, wire eel pot
hine   a young woman

Hine-nui-te-po [Hine-nui-te-pō] (Great woman of night) the Māori goddess of night and death, and the ruler of the underworld. When Māui attempted to make mankind immortal by crawling through her body while she slept, a laughing fantail woke her and she crushed him with her vagina, making him the first man to die. See also **Maui**, below

Hiruharama Jerusalem

Hoani John, generally referring to Baxter's son

Hone John

te ihi essential force, excitement, power, charm, personal magnetism – psychic force as opposed to spiritual power (mana)

inanga whitebait, the small silvery-whitefish native to New Zealand; a whitish or creamy-coloured variety of translucent greenstone

ka a particle used before a verb to name an event as occurring or a state existing. See **ka timata te pupuhi o te hau**, below

kahawai an edible greenish-blue to silvery-white schooling coastal fish with dark markings and spots, elongated body and a high front dorsal fin

kai food, meal

kaore [kāore] no

kaore nga pukapuka no books

karaka a large coastal tree with dark green, very glossy, large leaves and orange berries containing seeds which are poisonous unless roasted. Cultivated by Māori

karakia a prayer or chant

nga karakia mo Hemi te tutua [nga karakia mo Hemi te tūtūā] the prayers for James the nobody

kare a ripple; my dear

Te Kare an object of affection; Baxter's name for his wife, as is the next entry

Te Kare o Nga Wai Te Kare of the waters

kauri New Zealand's largest forest tree, highly prized for its timber. Found only in northern North Island, it is cone-bearing with a massive trunk and small, oblong, leathery leaves. Soot from burnt kauri gum is used by Māori for tattooing

kea an intelligent, large, bold endemic parrot, olive-green with scarlet underwings that lives mainly in the alpine regions of the South Island

kehua [kēhua] ghost; spirits that linger on earth after death and haunt the living

ki to, towards

kina sea egg, common sea urchin

ko introductory particle without an English equivalent, used to emphasise the subject. See **ko tenei te po**, below

koe   you

kono   [kōnae] a small food basket woven from flax

koro   elderly man, grandfather, grandad, grandpa – term of address to an older man

kua   an introductory word indicating past tense

kuia   revered elderly woman, grandmother, female elder

kumara   [kūmara] sweet potato

kuri   [kurī] dog

mako   a large, fast-moving oceanic shark with deep blue back and white underparts; the tooth of the mako shark is used as an ornament

makutu   [mākutu] spell, curse, witchcraft, magic, sorcery

manu   bird

manuka   [mānuka] tea-tree, a common native scrub bush which often grows in dense clumps. It has aromatic, prickly leaves, many small, white, pink or red flowers and medicinal properties

Maoritanga   [Māoritanga] Māori culture, practices and beliefs

marae   tribal meeting-ground; the open area in front of the meeting house [wharenui], where formal greetings and discussions take place. Often also used to include the complex of buildings around the marae

matai   [matai] black pine, a coniferous, long-lived native tree of lowland forest with small, narrow leaves arranged in two rows, hammer-marked trunk and pale timber. Ripe seed is a deep blue-black with a pale purplish bloom

mate   death, sickness

Maui   [Māui] a well-known character in Polynesian narratives, who performed a number of amazing feats. One of his exploits was to try to kill the Death Goddess by entering her body. See **Hine–nui–te–po**, above. The Fish of Māui is the North Island of New Zealand, which he hooked and hauled up from the sea bottom

mo   for

nga mokai   [ngā mōkai] servant, captive, slave or pet. Baxter generally uses this term when referring to members of his commune, to mean 'the fatherless ones'; it is a phrase sometimes applied to the youngest members of a family

moko   Māori tattoo on face or body

mutu   finished, completed

Kua mutu   in Māori, the last words of Christ on the Cross

nga   the (plural)

ngaio   a species of shrub or small tree found in the coastal regions of New Zealand

ngakau   [ngākau] thoughts, heart (i.e. emotions)

Ngati   [Ngāti] prefix to indicate a tribal group

Ngati-Hiruharama   the Jerusalem tribe, referring to members of Baxter's commune rather than to local Māori

Ngati Whatua   [Ngāti Whātua] Auckland tribal group of the area from Kaipara to Tāmaki-makau-rau

nui   large

o   of

pa   [pā] a Māori village, traditionally fortified

Pakeha   [Pākehā] a New Zealander of European descent

paraoa   [parāoa] bread, flour

paua   [pāua] the New Zealand native abalone, an edible mollusc with a multi-hued shell often used as decoration in Māori art

pia   beer

te po   night

pohutukawa   [pōhutukawa] an evergreen coastal tree found particularly in the north of New Zealand. It bears large, red flowers about Christmas time and has leaves which are velvety-white underneath

porangi   [pōrangi] to be insane, mad, crazy

puha   [pūhā] sowthistle, frequently used by the Māori as a vegetable

pukapuka   book, letters, paper, documents

pukeko   [pūkeko] the purple swamp hen – a deep blue-coloured bird with a black head and upperparts, a white undertail and a scarlet bill that inhabits wetlands, estuaries and damp pasture areas

punga   [ponga] tree-fern

pupuhi   blowing

Te Ra   [*from* Tama-nui-te-rā] personification and sacred name of the sun; by extension, the Judaeo-Christian God

te ra rite tonu te Atua   the sun who is like the Lord

rata   [rātā] either a large forest tree with crimson flowers and hard red timber, or the native scarlet rātā vine with orange-red flowers, mainly during winter

Te Rauparaha   the formidable Māori rangatira (chief) and warrior who led the Ngāti Toa tribe and took a leading part in the inter-tribal Musket Wars of the early 1800s

raupo   [raupō] bullrush

rimu   red pine, a tall coniferous tree with dark brown flaking bark, scale-

like prickly leaves and gracefully weeping branches
rite   like
riwai   [rīwai] potato
roimata   a tear (of crying)
roimata ua, roimata tangata   the tears of man fall like the rain
taipo   [taipō] goblin, spook, ghost, unwanted supernatural visitors not of human origin that haunt the living; a devil or demon
taku   my
taku ngakau ki a koe   [take ngākau ki a koe] I give my heart to you
Te Tama   boy, son, possibly by extension 'The Son of God'. Also a possible reference to 'Te Waka o Tama-rereti' (Tama-rereti's Canoe), a constellation in the shape of a huge canoe. Tautoru (Orion's Belt) forms the stern while the Tail of the Scorpion is the prow. Māhutonga (the Southern Cross) is the anchor and the Pointers (the two stars used to locate the Southern Cross) are Te Taura o te Waka o Tama-rereti (the anchor line)
Nga Tama Toa   Young Warriors, a militant 1970s protest group for Māori rights, with which Baxter sometimes associated
Tangaroa   the Māori god of the sea and fish
tangata   man
tangi   to cry, weep, or lament. Also used as a shortened form of tangi-hanga: funeral, rites for the dead
te tangi o te manu   the cry of the bird
taniko   [tāniko] an ornamental border made by finger weaving patterns with coloured thread, especially on cloaks and headbands
taniwha   (noun) water spirit, monster, chief, something or someone awesome. Taniwha take many forms, from logs to reptiles and whales and often live in lakes, rivers or the sea. They are often regarded as guardians by the people who live in their territory
tapu   sacred, prohibited, restricted, set apart, forbidden
te   the (singular)
tena koe   [tēnā koe] hello (speaking to one person); thank you
tenei   [tēnei] this
ko tenei te po   [ko tēnei te pō] this is the night (the title of a song)
terakihi   [tarakihi] a silver marine fish with a black band behind the head. Deep body and strongly compressed, with one long ray in the pectoral fin
timata   [tīmata] to begin
ka timata te pupuhi o te hau   [ka tīmata te pupuhi o te hau] the wind began blowing
toi-toi   [toetoe] a plant native to New Zealand which grows on sand dunes, on rocks and cliff faces, along streams and swamp edges. Long, grassy leaves have a fine edge and saw-like teeth, flowers are white, feathery,

arching plumes. Stems were used for **tukutuku** panels (see below)

totara [tōtara] a large forest tree with prickly, olive-green leaves. Trees are either male or female, with the female producing bright red fruit. The timber is popular for carving. The reddish-brown bark peels in long strips and can be used for the outside covering of 'pōhā' – a bag to hold preserved birds

tuakana Baxter uses this word to mean elder brother (of a male), but it can also mean elder sister (of a female), or cousin (of the same gender from a more senior branch of the family)

tuatara an endemic reptile with baggy skin and spines down the back resembling a large lizard, famous for having a vestigial third eye in the back of its head

tukutuku ornamental lattice-work, used particularly between carvings around the walls of meeting houses. Tukutuku panels consist of vertical stakes, horizontal rods, and flexible material, which form the pattern. Each of the traditional patterns has a name. For example, the pattern formed with stitches that fall vertically, like albatross tears, representing misfortune and disaster, is called 'roimata toroa'

te tuna [the] eel of various species

tutua [tūtūā] a nobody, person of low birth, commoner, ordinary person, slave

Wahi Ngaro [Wāhi Ngaro] the Void, Space (a term used in Māori creation chants)

wai water; who

ko wai koe? who are you?

nga wai waves

waiata song

He Waiata mo Taku Tangi Song for my Funeral-Ceremony

He Waiata mo Te Kare Song for Te Kare

weta [wētā] a large New Zealand insect resembling a fearsome grasshopper

Te Whaea mother or aunty; generally capitalised by Baxter to refer to the Virgin Mary

whare house

te whare kehua the haunted house

wharepuni the principal meeting house of a village, guest house, sleeping house

whiori tail

Te Whiore o te Kuri The Tail of the Dog

Te Whiro the Māori god of things associated with evil, darkness and, particularly for Baxter, death

Te Whiti   Te Whiti O Rongomai was born in Ngamotu, Taranaki, in 1830. A religious prophet and leader of the Te Ati Awa Tribe, he advocated a policy of passive resistance at the time of the confiscation of Taranaki lands by the Europeans. The community he established at Parihaka was destroyed by British troops in 1881. He died in 1907

Glossary of Selected Non-Māori Words

bach   a weekend or holiday cottage, especially at a beach or lakeside

bin   mental hospital, from slang 'the loony bin'

boobhead   a prison inmate, one conditioned to prison life

clink   jail (from the name of a London prison)

maimai   a temporary bush shelter often made from materials to hand; a shelter for duckshooters. Probably derives from Aboriginal Nyungar maya-maya, a shelter, but given the intended purpose of Baxter's shelter, it also has connotations of the Māori word mimi, 'urine'

wharfie   New Zealand and Australian term for a stevedore, dock worker

Select Bibliography

Major Publications by James K. Baxter

Principal Poetry Volumes and Broadsheets

Beyond the Palisade. Christchurch: Caxton Press, 1944. 2nd edition (ed. Paul Millar), Auckland: Oxford University Press, 1998

Blow, Wind of Fruitfulness. Christchurch: Caxton Press, 1948

Hart Crane, a poem. Sumner: Catspaw Press, 1948

Charm for Hilary. Christchurch: Catspaw Press, 1949

Poems Unpleasant (with Louis Johnson and Anton Vogt). Christchurch: Pegasus Press, 1952

The Fallen House. Christchurch: Caxton Press, 1953

Rapunzel. Wellington: no imprint, 1953

Lament for Barney Flanagan, licensee of the Hesperus Hotel. Wellington: no imprint, 1954

Traveller's Litany. Wellington: Handcraft Press, 1955

The Iron Breadboard: Studies in New Zealand Writing. Wellington: Mermaid Press, 1957

The Night Shift, poems on aspects of love (with Charles Doyle, Louis Johnson, Kendrick Smithyman). Wellington: Capricorn Press, 1957

Chosen Poems. Bombay: Konkan Institute of Arts and Sciences, 1958

In Fires of No Return: Selected Poems. London: Oxford University Press, 1958

Ballad of Calvary Street. Wellington: no imprint, 1960

Howrah Bridge and Other Poems. London: Oxford University Press, 1961

A Selection of Poetry. Wellington: *Poetry Magazine*, 1964

A Bucket of Blood for a Dollar. Christchurch: John Summers Bookshop, 1965

The Gunner's Lament. Wellington: no imprint, 1965

The Old Earth Closet. Wellington: Wai-te-ata Press, 1965

Pig Island Letters. London: Oxford University Press, 1966

A Small Ode on Mixed Flatting, elicited by the decision of the Otago University authorities to forbid this practice among students. Christchurch: Caxton Press, 1967

The Lion Skin. Dunedin: Bibliography Room, University of Otago, 1967

a death song for mr mouldybroke. Christchurch: John Summers, [1968]

Ballad of the Stonegut Sugar Works. Auckland: no imprint, 1969

The Rock Woman: Selected Poems. London: Oxford University Press, 1969

Jerusalem Sonnets: Poems for Colin Durning. Dunedin: Bibliography Room, University of Otago, 1970. Reprinted Wellington: Price Milburn, 1975

The Junkies and the Fuzz. Wellington: Wai-te-ata Press, 1970

Jerusalem Blues 2. Plimmerton: Bottle Press, 1971

Jerusalem Daybook. Wellington: Price Milburn, 1971. [Poems and Prose]

Autumn Testament: Poetry and Prose Journal. Wellington: Price Milburn, 1972. 2nd edition (ed. Paul Millar), Auckland: Oxford University Press, 1997

Four God Songs. Karori: Futuna Press, [1972]

Letter to Peter Olds. Dunedin: Caveman Press, 1972

Ode to Auckland and other poems. Dunedin: Caveman Press, 1972

Runes. London: Oxford University Press, 1973

Two Obscene Poems. Adelaide: Mary Martin Books, 1973

The Labyrinth: Some Uncollected Poems 1944–72. Chosen by J.E. Weir. Wellington: Oxford University Press, 1974

The Tree House and Other Poems for Children. Wellington: Price Milburn, 1974

The Bone Chanter: Unpublished Poems 1945–72. Chosen and introduced by J.E. Weir. Wellington: Oxford University Press, 1976

The Holy Life and Death of Concrete Grady: Various Uncollected and Unpublished Poems. Chosen and introduced by J.E. Weir. Wellington: Oxford University Press, 1976

Collected Poems. Ed. J.E. Weir. Wellington: Oxford University Press, 1980. Includes a number of previously unpublished or uncollected poems. Reprinted with corrections 1981. Paperback 1988. Reissued in hardback with index, 1995

Selected Poems. Ed. J.E. Weir. Auckland: Oxford University Press, 1982

Cold Spring. Ed. Paul Millar. Auckland: Oxford University Press, 1996

New Selected Poems. Ed. Paul Millar. Auckland: Oxford University Press, 2001. Reprinted 2004

Selected Other Works

Recent Trends in New Zealand Poetry. Christchurch: Caxton Press, 1951. [Criticism]

The Fire and the Anvil: Notes on Modern Poetry. Wellington: New Zealand University Press, 1955. [Criticism]

Aspects of Poetry in New Zealand. Christchurch: Caxton Press, 1967. [Criticism]

The Man on the Horse. Dunedin: University of Otago Press, 1967. [Criticism and some poetry]

The Flowering Cross. Dunedin: *New Zealand Tablet*, 1969. [Prose and some poetry]

Thoughts about the Holy Spirit. Wellington: Futuna Press, 1973. [Prose and some poetry]

James K. Baxter as Critic: A Selection from his Literary Criticism. Ed. Frank McKay. Auckland: Heinemann Educational Books, 1978

Collected Plays. Ed. Howard McNaughton. Auckland: Oxford University Press, 1982

Horse. Auckland: Oxford University Press, 1985. [Novella]

Selected Studies of Baxter's Life and Work

Doyle, Charles. *James K. Baxter*. Boston: Twayne Publishers, 1976

McKay, Frank. *The Life of James K. Baxter*. Auckland: Oxford University Press, 1990

Millar, Paul. *Spark to a Waiting Fuse: James K. Baxter's Correspondence with Noel Ginn, 1942–46*. Wellington: Victoria University Press, 2001

Newton, John. *The Double Rainbow: James K Baxter, Ngati Hau and the Jerusalem Commune*. Wellington: Victoria University Press, 2009

Oliver, W.H. *James K. Baxter: A Portrait*. Auckland: Godwit Press / Bridget Williams Books, 1994

O'Sullivan, Vincent. *James K. Baxter*. Wellington: Oxford University Press, 1976

Weir, J.E. *The Poetry of James K. Baxter*. Wellington: Oxford University Press, 1970

Bibliography

Weir, J.E. and Barbara A. Lyon (eds), *A Preliminary Bibliography of Works by and about James K. Baxter*. Christchurch: University Canterbury (NZ), 1979

Index of Titles

Index of First Lines